THE PHYSIOLOGY OF BRASS PLAYING

JOHN RIDGEON

John Ridgeon was born in Barking in 1944. He studied trumpet at the Royal Academy of Music during which time he developed a particular interest in the physical aspects of brass playing. His work as a player, teacher and researcher in this field has led to the publication of a series of books which have become standard works in the brass library.

His lecture tours have taken him to Australia, Japan and the USA in addition to his schedule in Britain, Europe and Scandinavia.

One of the most challenging aspects of his career is consultation work with professional brass players. This brings together his three main areas of interest; music, teaching and physiology of brass playing.

In education John Ridgeon has had appointments as Supervising Brass Teacher for the London Borough of Redbridge, Instrumental Organiser for the London Borough of Barnet and Senior Music Adviser for Leicestershire. He established and directed the Instrumental Teaching Course at the Guildhall School of Music and Drama and was Chairman of the National Association of Brass Teachers in Education. In 1986 he organised the annual conference of the International Trum-pet Guild which brought to London some of the world's finest players and teachers of trumpet.

Since 1986 John Ridgeon has devoted his time increasingly to the training of professional musicians in working in education and the wider community, establishing Access to Music which has rapidly become accepted as a leading organisation in this field.

In 1991 he was made an Associate of the Royal Academy of Music for his outstanding services to music.

© 1986 Brass Wind Educational Supplies and Co.
All rights reserved. No part of this publication may be reproduced, stored in a retrieval system or transmitted in any form or by any means, electronic, mechanical, photocopying, recording or otherwise without the prior permission of Brass Wind Educational Supplies and Co.

CONTENTS

DEDICATED TO THE MEMORY OF
PHIL PARKER SNR.

INTRODUCTION

What makes a natural or instinctive player? The definition of instinct is intuition, which is in turn defined as an immediate mental apprehension without reasoning. Instinctive players are particularly observant and can apprehend merely by watching others around them. Players who do not have the same visual sensibility but who are equally musical, can achieve the same or similar results. This may take longer to accomplish but if the correct physiological approach is established through a reasoned process the muscular memory which is intrinsic to skill will be developed.

This book attempts to aid an understanding of the physiology of brass playing so that players can use the knowledge to further develop their own skills or pass on this understanding to their students.

John Ridgeon

1 BREATHING

"Why interfere with the instinctive behaviour of breathing?" I have been asked this question on many occasions and have always felt justified in responding with another question. "Why express surprise at the notion of modified breathing, even though it is not natural, when the bodily function of speaking and singing interfere with passive respiration?"

> *Respiration is essentially an automatic act that can be modified but not repressed by voluntary control. Accordingly, the respiratory act for voice is a modified, often greatly altered, form of the primary mechanism.*
>
> *Robert Curry, The Mechanism of the Human Voice, Pub: Churchill Ltd. 1940. J and A Churchill.*

We should therefore examine the way in which passive breathing is modified by wind players in order to produce an extended musical phrase. An awareness of this differential will advance the effectiveness of breath support and help the performer return to passive breathing when not playing. This is most important, because just as passive breathing is inappropriate for wind playing, so is 'overbreathing' inappropriate for the more normal bodily activities. The inability to return to gentle, passive breathing frequently results in the wind player hyper ventilating.

> *Habitual hyperventilation is a common cause for referring patients to a cardiologist with the suspicion of angina ... The past history may offer clues to the over breathing tendancy or habit. For example, swimmers and athletes may have learned to hyperventilate as an aid to performance, and the training of singers, wind instrumentalists and military personnel encourages thoracic breathing and thus puts them at special risk.*
>
> *D. W. Evans, MD and L. C. Lum, MB, Hyperventilation as a Cause of Angina-like Pain, Practical Cardiology, Med Publishing Inc.*

As the breath is the motivator of a wind player's sound and the expressive source of musicianship, I make no apology for discussing this aspect of performance in some detail. The following is a simple description of our breathing apparatus which should help in understanding its functions during wind playing.

THE PHYSIOLOGY

The 'thoracic cavity', commonly known as the chest, contains the lungs, and is enclosed by the ribs. It is separated from the abdomen by a domed shaped diaphragm which is attached to the lower, back ribs and the back bone.

A change in the size of the chest causes a change in the air pressure in the lungs. During inhalation, the air pressure is reduced below that of the atmosphere, causing air to flow into the lungs until atmospheric pressure is resumed. During exhalation the air pressure is increased and air is forced out until once again the pressure is restored to atmospheric for the start of the next inhalation.

Two actions encourage changes in the size of the chest:

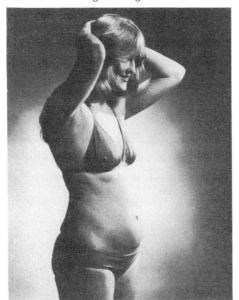 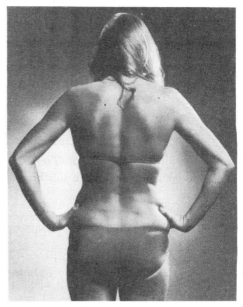

■ The diaphragm contracts downwards, deepening the cavity. Beneath it are the abdominal contents which have to be lowered to make space.

 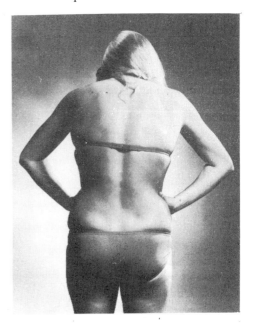

■ The ribs are raised to increase the breadth of the cavity by means of the intercostal (rib) muscles. These are divided into external and internal groups. During passive breathing no distinction can be made between the function of these groups, but for wind playing, a more defined role becomes apparent. The external muscles are known to raise the ribs on inhalation and the internal muscles to lower the ribs on exhalation.

For passive inhalation, sufficient breath can be ventilated by diaphragmatic or rib contraction. For wind playing, however, most would use a combination of these activities. The proportion would vary from instrument to instrument.

When relaxed, exhalation is largely a matter of releasing the muscles employed for inhalation. The diaphragm and the ribs return to their passive position through the elasticity of the lungs and the tendons of the diaphragm. The diaphragm cannot contract in an upwards direction on exhalation. For wind playing, breathing out is supported by employing the abdominal muscles to forcefully return the diaphragm to its passive position.

So much for theory. Let us now discuss its practical application to brass playing.

In order to present the broadest possible spectrum of opinion, I have included the thoughts of players and teachers collected over a number of years during visits to different countries. In particular I undertook an extensive survey of opinion in universities and conservatoires throughout North America.

INHALATION

Question 1	Answers	
Do you advise a student to 'push out' or 'flop' the abdominal muscles when inhaling?	Push out	80%
	Flop	10%
	Leave it to the student	10%

Comment: The words 'push out' concern me although I recognise that this suggestion can help some students. I believe that many, however, are misguided by the implications.

The physiological requirement is to achieve a relaxed abdominal wall which allows the contents to fall to the bottom of the cavity. This makes room for the diaphragm to contract downwards.

It is easy to see how the words 'push out' have come into general use. The player senses the diaphragmatic *push* and sees the abdominal wall come *out*. The resulting instruction is 'push out'. I have found that students respond to this instruction by tensing their abdomens, thereby packing the abdominal contents beneath the diaphragm. This restricts the free movement down into the abdominal cavity.

The word 'flop', however, encourages a relaxed mental and therefore physical approach. The tummy muscles relax forward allowing the stomach and other organs to take a lower position in the abdomen. This leaves the diaphragm free to contract downwards.

Any player experiencing tension on inhalation should re-examine this inhalation procedure.

Question 2	Answers	
Do you teach a student to:		
Maintain a permanently raised chest?		10%
Maintain a permanently passive chest?		10%
Expand the chest during inhalation?		80%

Comment: Players who choose to maintain a permanently raised chest during inhalation claim to find this the best way of liberating the diaphragm. There is little doubt that considerable diaphragm freedom is achieved. However I do find that fatigue becomes apparent over a prolonged period of playing because of the permanently contracted intercostal muscles. Nevertheless, I recommend this manner of breathing to a player who carries an excess of body weight. In this case the fatty tissue inhibits the free movement of the diaphragm. Holding the chest permanently erect dissipates the unwanted tissue.

Those who advocate a passive chest during inhalation attempt to avoid a problem experienced by some excessive chest breathers—a comparatively small inhalation in exchange for an inordinately large chest movement. I sympathise with the motive but arrive at a different solution. I believe that a student experiences this scarcity of air when he reverses his normal breathing pattern. Usually, on inhalation, the upper chest is the last area to expand following the diaphragm and the lower rib cage. The tidal flow reverts to exhalation after the upper rib cage is raised. It is possible, therefore, that when a player deliberately *starts* with an upper chest expansion, the instinctive urge is to abandon diaphragmatic contraction in favour of the exhalation element in the sequence. This would, of course, severely limit the volume of inhalation. This does not apply to those players who *finish* their inhalation with a raised chest.

Those who advocate chest expansion during inhalation, normally recommend this when an extra large breath is required. You will note that their motive appears to be the antithesis of the passive chest advocators. Their aim is to start inhalation with a diaphragmatic contraction or a combination of diaphragm and lower chest contraction and finish inhalation with a lifting of the upper chest. For small breaths the diaphragm and lower rib cage would be used. For large breaths the upper rib cage would be expanded as well. An example of this is the tuba player who would use more upper chest movement than the piccolo trumpet player.

I encourage my students to adopt the following sequence:

- Relax the abdominal wall so that the abdominal contents drop to the bottom of the cavity.
- Smoothly, lower the diaphragm to start the inhalation.
- Sense the diaphragm pulling the lower ribs into action.
- Raise the upper chest from the sternum.
- Incorporate all contractions into one flowing movement for quick breaths.

Sometimes a student will have difficulties in combining these movements. If so, a brisk run around the campus will give a natural experience of the sensation. Alternatively, sit the student on a chair with his legs apart; push the trunk of the body down until the tummy presses against the insides of the thighs. Clasp the pupil's lower ribs and ask him to inhale. This also should heighten an awareness of the necessity to expand in areas which have been restricted.

EXHALATION

Question 3	Answers	
Do you advise a student to support his lip vibration with diaphragmatic or abdominal contraction?	Diaphragmatic	20%
	Abdominal	40%
	Show by example	40%

Comment: Most of my interviewees that suggested using the diaphragm to support a forceful exhalation admitted that they were merely utilizing terminology which was first introduced to them by their teachers. Few considered that the advice would stand up to physiological examination but considered it adequate for the purpose.

A number of those who recommended abdominal support had a thorough knowledge of the physiology involved. Others had a less detailed understanding but all in this group considered abdominal control fundamental to good brass playing.

Those who showed by example were not concerned with terminology as they considered that a student learns best through observation.

The physiological explanation contains two pertinent statements which relate to this question.

- The diaphragm returns to its passive position through the elasticity of the tendons. It cannot contract in an upward direction on exhalation.
- For wind playing, breathing out is supported by employing the abdominal muscles to forcefully return the diaphragm to its passive position.

As it is a physiological impossibility to contract the diaphragm in an upwards direction, any suggestion of diaphragmatic support is incorrect.

To recommend abdominal support promotes the correct physiological information.

To show by examples is correct so far as the student can see. Unfortunately, the more complex contractions are quite invisible. Communicating successfully therefore depends upon the teacher's skill in creating mental images with words.

It may appear from the above that the diaphragm has no part to play in exhalation. This is not so. I have learned that the diaphragm does, in fact, have a major role to play but that the nature of this role is contrary to popular belief.

4

2   THE PRIMARY RESISTER

Having mastered the mechanics of inhalation and exhalation the next logical step is to find the means of extending an exhalation in order to support a phrase and create an acceptable tone colour.

Consider a beginner. The exhalation is invariably uncontrolled resulting in a sound recognised as being typical of this stage. How is control often achieved? Many beginners simply experiment until a tone, adequate to satisfy immediate needs, is produced. Some are fortunate and arrive at a physically correct solution which will be the foundation of future technique, but the majority simply stumble on a temporary means of coping with early demands. Unfortunately, this normally results in some form of muscle abuse which will require remedial work at a later stage. Working from the basis that it is easier to learn than relearn, I prefer to encourage a beginner to work methodically towards controlled exhalation. The problem lies in finding a suitable vehicle for experiencing the correct breathing sensations to which the theory can be related. An instrument is normally a hinderance in achieving this as the novice is inclined to tense his breathing apparatus when playing. However, I have found singing to be enormously helpful as an aid for the beginner in sensing exhalation control.

Ask a novice to sing a long, soft note or a group of very short notes. Get him to repeat this several times with one hand on the lower ribs and the other hand on the middle of the tummy. Ask him to close his eyes. I have found this a help in focusing attention. The principle sensation to be located by the pupil is the 'semi-locking' reaction which makes an extended exhalation possible and shortens the end of a note. Experiment further by singing high, low and loud notes. A non-musical way of experiencing this locking reaction is through lifting a heavy weight. In this instance the 'lock' is total.

Some students are most insensitive to these feelings and are unable to recognise the 'locking' reaction when it occurs. In these circumstances, it is important to develop a general physical awareness before working on specific brass techniques. The following suggestions can help:

- Sense the blood flowing through the body.
- Sense the heart beating.
- Twitch the end of the nose.
- Move the ears.
- Move the scalp.
  .... and so on.

Having heightened this physical awareness focus attention on some normal breathing patterns and relate these to the demands of playing.

The deep inhalation with a 'hold' before exhalation   Sometimes required in preparation for a loud attack.

- Sense the sudden relaxation of the abdominal wall.
- Sense the abdominal contents falling to the bottom of the abdominal cavity.
- Sense the diaphragmatic contraction thrusting downwards into the cavity.
- Sense the 'locking' of the diaphragm's tendons.
- Sense the preparatory contractions of the abdominal muscles ready for exhalation.

The forceful exhalation required for a loud attack

- Sense the power of the abdominal thrust.
- Sense the abdominal organs being forced upwards.
- Sense the release of the diaphragm.

The slow release required for soft playing

- Sense the distinct 'locking' or holding sensation at the end of the inhalation and at the beginning of the exhalation.
- Sense the progressive relaxation of the diaphragm.
- Sense the abdominal muscles maintaining a steady air pressure.

You will have noticed a constant reference to the 'locking' sensation. This important facet of control is known as antagonistic contraction and is the primary means of achieving a controlled exhalation necessary to support the extended phrase.

Questions 4–8 will explore the method by which antagonistic contraction is developed together with its uses.

Do you teach antagonistic contraction of the abdominal muscles and the diaphragm in order to control an extended phrase?

Only a few of my interviewees responded to the question presented in this form. The answers apply to the following adaptation:

Question 4	Answers	
When playing an extended phrase do you sense a 'locking' sensation located in the diaphragm/upper abdominal region?	Yes	68%
	No	32%

Comment: The large majority of my interviewees were aware of a 'locking' sensation whilst playing. Most agreed that the sensation felt like two sets of muscles contracting against each other, but because of uncertainty as to the exact physiological function, any detailed talk about this aspect of playing was avoided.

The remainder of my interviewees were unaware of a 'locking' sensation. On examination, some discovered that they had subconsciously incorporated this technique into their playing whilst others considered that a withholding of breath was the antithesis of good brass playing.

As has been stated the fundamental function of 'locking' the breathing muscles is to enable a player to extend a breath for the duration of a musical phrase. This is done by resisting a rapid exhalation which would otherwise follow an unimpeded contraction of the abdominal muscles. This 'locking' sensation is the contraction of the diaphragm as it pushes downward against the upward thrust of the abdominal muscles. Push one hand against the other. You will sense a similar feeling.

The pressure of the air column causes you to feel that you are leaning or pressing against the higher position of the diaphragm and abdominal regions. In other words, there is one force on the outside pressing inwards and upwards, and one force on the inside pressing outward and downward. The two forces pressing against one another create tension, and this causes the so called 'locking' of the diaphragm.

Donald S. Reinhard, *Pivot System*, Elkan-Vogal Inc./UMP Ltd.

Question 5	Answers	
Do you advise a student to make staccato notes using the tongue, or glottis or by terminating the breath?	Tongue	0%
	Glottis	0%
	Breath	100%

Comment: Whilst my interviewees recognised that it is possible to stop notes using the tongue or glottis they rejected the tongue for being an unmusical form of note stopping and rejected the glottis for fear of developing throat tension. It was unanimously agreed that staccato notes were best stopped 'on the breath' in order to produce the most musical results.

Question 6	Answers	
When you make staccato notes by terminating the breath, do you sense a 'locking' of the breathing muscles?	Yes	68%
	No	32%

Comment: A contradiction occurs with 32% claiming not to sense the 'locking' of the breathing muscles. I believe that it is impossible to stop the breath quickly solely by terminating the contraction of the abdominal muscles. Some kind of resistance has to interrupt the exhalation abruptly. If the tongue and the glottis are rejected, then, in my opinion, resistance must be created by the downward contraction of the diaphragm which interrupts the abdominal exhalation; the antagonistic contraction. I have found the following analogy a useful way of illustrating to students the necessity for using antagonistic contraction instead of an ugly tongue stop in staccato playing:

- Imagine kicking a ball. On impact the resistance of the ball is sufficient to prevent the leg from swinging too far. This is an equivalent of the tongue being used like an 'air brake' to stop the breath.
- What happens if the ball is removed just prior to impact? Surely the leg would continue to swing? This is an equivalent of the tongue being prevented from stopping the note. The breath would continue to exhale resulting in failure to achieve a staccato.
- Imagine the same happening again but this time the leg is prevented from swinging too far by a length of string tied to the foot. This is an equivalent of stopping the breath by contracting the diaphragm downwards in antagonistic contraction to the abdominal muscles.

It is interesting that many of those who are conscious of antagonistic contraction during staccato playing choose not to highlight its significance in a teaching situation. Two main reasons are given:

- The desired contractions are accomplished automatically due to the student's drive for musical excellence.
- A clear explanation is difficult to present particularly to a younger student.

Try the following with younger students if an 'every day' analogy is required:

John Ridgeon, Scene 1 for the Brass Player, Brass Wind Educational Supplies

Question 7	Answers	
Do you encourage the use of a 'locking' sensation of the breathing muscles for soft and, in particular, high, soft playing?	Yes	68%
	No	32%

Comment: The response from my interviewees was identical to that of Question 6. I therefore intend to reflect my own views in these comments. I have been asked on many occasions to convince people who play instinctively that they have adopted antagonistic contraction as part of their technique. So, if you are an instinctive player and are uncertain whether or not you sense antagonistic contraction when playing high, soft notes—try this:

■ Select a music excerpt that is pitched in the medium to high register and marked 'p'. Follow your normal inhalation routine and allow this to progress to the moment of articulation. As soon as the note has been sounded, pull the mouthpiece away from your embouchure. The sudden release of air which you experience results from the unlocking of the breathing muscles. This allows the now unwanted air pressure to dissipate. You will recollect identical sensations when conductors have aborted entries of similar passages.

What in physiological terms is happening, and why does it happen? Well, in the first place, brass players must generate air pressure to support a lip vibration. Without adequate air pressure the lips will either vibrate erratically or stop vibrating altogether. Clearly, less pressure is demanded for soft playing but this should not be achieved by reducing the abdominal support to a minimum. If this is done the result is insecure playing since the abdominal muscles used by themselves lack the sensitivity to respond to minute lip variations. The following quote from Farkas lends emphasis to this point:

Perhaps before considering the various points of resistance, this is a good time to warn of a bad habit prevalent among wind players which is particularly detrimental to their soft playing and which again points up the need for resistance somewhere. The general pressure of abdomen and intercostal muscles can be made very light resulting in an exhalation of little 'push'. In my opinion, this principle of using very little pressure from the diaphragm for the production of soft volume is a serious error . . . . The real danger of blowing a brass instrument incorrectly occurs during soft passages. At such times, the player has the choice of simply pushing very lightly with the diaphragm and letting the air drift through the open unresisting passage or of pushing quite firmly with the diaphragm, but holding back this stronger air-column to the desired volume by resisting the air somewhere.

Philip Farkas, *The Art of Brass Playing, Wind Music Inc.,*

You will have noticed some points of similarity between this quote and my previous comments. However, there is one significant difference. Farkas refers to the diaphragm in addition to the abdominal and intercostal muscles as generators of air pressure on exhalation, whereas I would refer predominantly to the abdominal muscles in this role with the intercostal muscles used in a very subsidiary capacity (see Question 3). It is interesting to note that in an earlier publication, The Art of Horn Playing (1956), Farkas says:

*This combination of effort gives the controlled pressure we need. By far the most important of these two pressures is the one caused by contraction of the waist muscles. This is often referred to as 'diaphragm pressure'. The expression is a misnomer, however, as the diaphragm does its **real work** on the inhalation and is **relaxed** on the exhalation, regardless of the heavy pressure being put upon it from underneath.*

Summy Birchard Music Copyright © 1956 Birch Tree Group Ltd. Used by permission.

In view of this, it is safe to assume the comment "using very little pressure from the diaphragm" actually referred to the diaphragm creating air pressure by relaxing against the thrust from the "heavy pressure being put upon it from underneath".

8

<table>
<tr><td>Question 8</td><td colspan="2">Answers</td></tr>
<tr><td rowspan="3">Do you advise a student to vary the position of antagonistic contraction in accordance with register?</td><td>Yes</td><td>100%</td></tr>
<tr><td>No</td><td>0%</td></tr>
<tr><td colspan="2">N.B. These answers apply to those interviewees that sense antagonistic contraction.</td></tr>
</table>

Comment: Advice seems to be restricted to the statement 'raise the abdomen for high notes and lower abdomen for low notes'. In my opinion, this is perfectly adequate when reinforced by a demonstration, such as a push in the appropriate region! The following comments are for those interested in a more detailed explanation:

The amount of air in the lungs dictates the degree of air pressure and the position of the antagonistic contraction. The fuller the lungs the lower will be the starting point of the contraction.

When a note sequence moves up, the air pressure has to be increased. This requires a raising of the 'floor beneath the lungs so that the air is compressed to well above atmospheric pressure. This in turn forces the breath from the lungs at a rapid rate. This rapid exhalation is required for loud, high notes. However, it is inappropriate for soft, high notes. In this instance, the increased air pressure is required but not the rapid release of breath. To avoid this, the diaphragm resists the abdominal contraction.

When a note sequence moves down, the air pressure has to be decreased. This requires a lowering of the 'floor' beneath the lungs which rarefies the air and results in a slower exhalation. Again, if a loud note is required the abdominal muscles contract unresisted but if a soft note is required, the diaphragm works in antagonistic contraction.

Question 9

What analogy, if any, do you use to encourage a good breathing habit?

Think of the lungs as a bottle. Liquid flows to the bottom first and then rises to the top. The same must apply when filling the lungs.

The popularity of this analogy reflects the importance placed by brass teachers on the correct sequence of inhalation. Diaphragm first followed by intercostal inhalation.

Think of the lungs as a balloon – When inflated the air escapes from the open teat due to the elasticity of the material. However, if the teat hole is reduced by pulling on either side, the elasticity of the balloon is insufficient to expel the air. In order for this to be accomplished, it is necessary to squeeze the balloon under one's arm. In so doing, the two surfaces vibrate around the opening and produce a note of determined pitch. The note can then be varied by increasing or decreasing the arm pressure in relation to the resistance of the teat.

The similarity to the brass player's physiology is striking. When the lips are contracted to form an aperture, the elasticity of the lungs and diaphragm is no longer sufficient to expel the air. However, by utilizing the abdominal muscles, the lips can be excited into vibration. The note achieved can then be varied by increasing or decreasing the abdominal pressure in relation to the resistance of the player's lips.

Inhale a ball and exhale a thread

This third analogy is pithy but cogent and emphasises the importance of resistance in breathing.

. . . . Compare your breathing apparatus to a pipe organ. The longer the pipe and the longer the opening, the lower the note; as the pipe becomes shorter and the opening smaller, the pitch becomes higher. Therefore, the longer the notes you play, the longer the air column. . . . In our brass playing for the low

9

register you should make your inhalation a normal breath, slightly protruding the entire abdominal region. . . . For the middle register the diaphragm should take a slight inward and upward position. . . . For the top register the diaphragm and abdominal regions mover very much in and up.

Donald S. Reinhardt, Pivot System, Elkan-Vogel Inc./UMP Ltd.

.

3 RESISTANCE AT THE GLOTTAL APERTURE, 'THE VOLUME CONTROLLER'

Three factors have been mentioned by Reinhardt to which I would add resistance at the glottal aperture. This is the next area of resistance to the breath on leaving the lungs. The glottal aperture together with the mouth aperture (Chapter 4), and the lip aperture (Chapter 5), controls the quantity, speed and direction of the expired breath. Each area has a specific role to play but is interdependent. I call these "subsidiary resisters" to the primary means by which we control exhalation, the antagonistic contraction of the diaphragm and abdominal muscles.

ANATOMICAL DESCRIPTION OF THE GLOTTAL APERTURE

This aperture between the vocal chords is part of the larynx and is situated at the top of the trachea. The glottis is used in a variety of ways to control phonation during speech and singing, and to help the breathing muscles regulate the amount of air leaving the lungs. When the breathing muscles push air upwards against the resisting larynx muscles, breath pressure is created.

The anatomy of the larynx is most complex but for the purpose of this treatise I only intend to refer to the muscles that cause a state of antagonistic contraction in the vocal chords. These are the twin "cricoartenoid porticus" which produce a state of variable balance of the glottal aperture as in sounding "h" or as in laboured breathing.

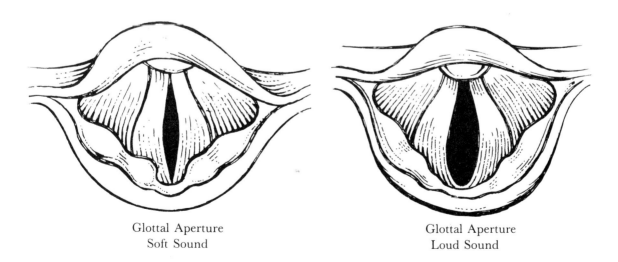

| Glottal Aperture | Glottal Aperture |
| Soft Sound | Loud Sound |

■ Whisper a long "h——". Sense the antagonistic contraction of the twin cricoartenoid porticus muscles in the vocal chords.

11

Also sense the antagonistic contraction of the diaphragm and abdominal muscles. These two sets of muscles co-ordinate their efforts for the normal body behaviour of whispering.

This same co-ordinated effort is required by the brass player in order to produce a soft, secure sound.

- Relax the muscles in your vocal chords and forcefully breathe "ha". Sense the opening of the vocal chords which increases the glottal aperture as in yawning.

Also sense the relaxation of the diaphragm. This co-ordinated withdrawal of resistance to breath exhalation leaves the "channel" wide open and free for the abdominal muscles to rapidly force out air.

This same co-ordinated withdrawal of resistance is required by the brass player in order to produce a loud, free sound.

These two examples are extremes which encompass an infinite number of variable muscular contractions. When the brass player achieves a conscious co-ordination of the glottal aperture and the breath musculature, he will be able to control the vibrating lip tissue and develop a wide, secure dynamic range. Hence the subtitle, "The Volume Controller".

Question 10	Answers	
Do you personally sense breath resistance at the glottis according to volume?:	Yes	60%
	No	40%

Question 11	Answers	
If you do this, do you also encourage a student to sense glottal breath resistance according to volume?	Yes	35%
	No	65%

Comment: The dichotomy experienced by teachers when dealing with this area of resistance results from a fundamental misunderstanding of the physiological role of the glottis. Many of the interviewees answering "Yes" to Question 10 while also answering "No" to Question 11 have attempted to eradicate glottal breath resistance from their own playing, and have done so in the belief that it is detrimental to good tone production. This explains the apparent contradiction between the answers to Questions 10 and 11. Investigation into the cause for concern heightens another function of the glottis.

THE GLOTTAL APERTURE AS A SAFETY VALVE

Again ■ Whisper "h——" and sense the closing of the glottal aperture.
   ■ Forcefully breathe "ha" and sense the opening of the aperture.

I re-emphasize that in order to achieve a forceful exhalation suitable for a loud note, withdrawal of glottal and breath resistance is required. However, if this forceful supply of air is unable to escape through a lip aperture which is too small or badly aligned, the air will reverse in direction and build pressure until the glottis is forced into a partial closure. This closing is an involuntary action, a "safety valve", which helps to restrict the pressure within the head cavity to an acceptable level by monitoring the amount of breath entering the head from the chest cavity. The result is an unpleasant explosive sensation experienced in the throat. No matter how much effort the player devotes to removing this "blockage" the problem will remain.

Frustration causes a further reduction of the lip aperture and so forth into a descending spiral.

Correct the fault at the lip aperture and the problem of a reduced glottal aperture for loud playing will be most often, involuntarily resolved.

DEVELOPMENT OF SENSITIVITY TO THE GLOTTAL APERATURE

I have already mentioned the need of a brass player to reproduce the normal bodily functions of the glottis, so I encourage students to spend some time focusing on this part of the anatomy. Correct behaviour will be recorded in muscular memory through repetition. This behaviour can then be reproduced instinctively in response to musical stimuli.

- The glottal aperture is completely closed when:
  Lifting a heavy weight.
  Straining.
- The glottal aperture is wide open when:
  Panting after running fast.
  Blowing out candles
  Yawning.
- The glottal aperture is partially open when:
  Whispering.
  Blowing gently.
- The glottal aperture is closed but bursts open when:
  Coughing.
  Spitting.
  Sneezing.
- The glottal aperture is open but closes when:
  Hiccuping.

Repeat these functions regularly until the sensations are recognized. Note the co-ordination of the glottal aperture and the breathing muscles.

FUNCTIONS OF THE GLOTTAL APERTURE IN RELATION TO BRASS PLAYING

Try transferring this sensitivity to volume control on an instrument. Perform the appropriate body function before playing each musical exercise. You will know when the breathing muscles and the glottal aperture are properly balanced by the quality and security of the sound.

- The glottal aperture can be completely closed when suddenly stopping the breath. This co-ordinates with and is subsidiary to antagonistic contraction of the breathing muscles.

- The glottal aperture is wide open when playing loudly. This co-ordinates with a relaxation of the diaphragm and a strong contraction of the abdominal muscles. Make certain that you maintain an adequate lip aperture. Otherwise, the breath flow will reverse and cause "back-pressure" which will reduce the glottal aperture.

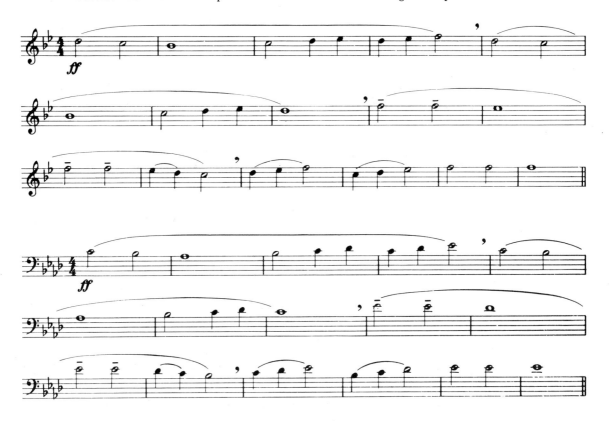

- The glottal aperture is partially open when playing softly. This co-ordinates with a firm but not violent antagonistic contraction of the breathing muscles.

14

- Now try the previous exercise up a fifth. You will discover the increased antagonistic contraction of the breathing muscles and the corresponding support from the glottal aperture. This sensitivity to the role results in soft playing which is confident and secure.

- The glottal aperture starts small but opens progressively when playing a crescendo. This co-ordinates with an antagonistic contraction of the breath muscles, followed by a progressive relaxation of the diaphragm which allows the abdominal muscles freedom to strengthen the exhalation.

- The glottal aperture starts large but reduces progressively when playing a diminuendo. This co-ordinates with a forceful contraction of the abdominal muscles and a passive diaphragm. The glottal aperture reduces as the diaphragm becomes active against a reduced abdominal contraction.

- Notice that the antagonistic contraction of the breathing muscles is more obvious when playing high.

4 RESISTANCE AT THE MOUTH APERTURE, 'THE RANGE CONTROLLER'

The mouth aperture supports the breathing muscles by regulating the speed and direction of air and, in so doing, establishes the general range of notes within which the lips will most effectively vibrate. This aperture is the next area of subsidiary resistance after the breath has left the glottal aperture.

ANATOMICAL DESCRIPTION OF THE MOUTH APERTURE

The perimeter of the mouth aperture includes the upper and lower sets of teeth, the hard palate, the soft palate and the lower jaw. Within the mouth aperture lies the tongue which is attached to the lower jaw by the "genioglossus muscle". The tongue and lower jaw regulate the size of the mouth aperture.

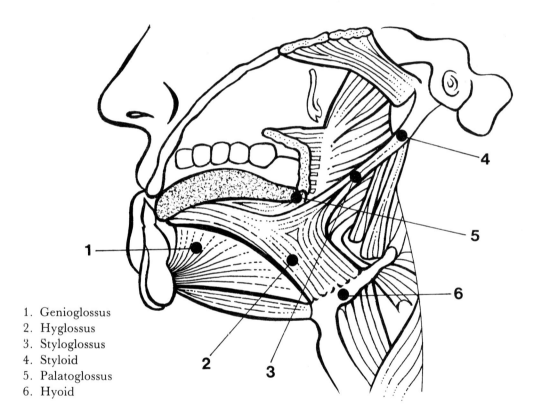

1. Genioglossus
2. Hyglossus
3. Styloglossus
4. Styloid
5. Palatoglossus
6. Hyoid

The Tongue   The muscles of the tongue fall into two groups.

(a) Extrinsic muscles which join the tongue to the jaw, skull and hyoid bone.

   The genioglossus
   ■ Withdraws and protrudes the tongue and raises the dorsum.
   ■ Joins the whole tongue, tip and root to the lower jaw.

   The hyoglosus
   ■ Flattens the sides of the tongue.
   ■ Joins the sides of the tongue to the hyoid bone.

17

The styloglossus
- Retracts and elevates the sides of the tongue causing a concavity of the dorsum.
- Joins the outside of the tongue along its entire length to the styloid bone.

The palatoglossus
- Elevates the tongue and depresses the soft palate.
- Joins the back of the tongue to the anterior palate.

(b) Intrinsic muscles which are situated within the tongue and are accessories to the extrinsic muscles.

The lingualis
- Consists of longitudinal fibres within the tongue.

The transversus
- Consists of transverse fibres within the tongue.

The perpendicularis
- Consists of vertical fibres within the tongue.

These intrinsic muscles co-ordinate to affect the overall texture of the tongue and to control movement at the tip of the tongue.

The Lower Jaw   The construction of the lower jaw allows for horizontal and vertical movement. Imagine biting .... the lower jaw thrusts forward and moves down, bites and is then withdrawn. In this withdrawn position the molars are aligned in order to masticate the food. The horizontal movement of the lower jaw has a great influence over the structure of the embouchure. It is of fundamental importance that the correct position is selected during the first instrumental lesson. Failure to achieve this creates a weak foundation on which to form the embouchure, which in turn distorts the free flow of breath.

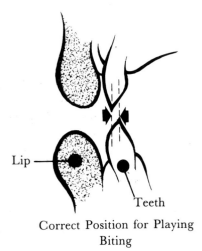

Correct Position for Playing
Biting

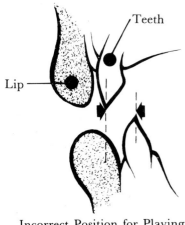

Incorrect Position for Playing
Masticating

Most young beginners fail to achieve the correct "biting" position for two reasons;

- The jaw is in its resting position when set back. Sustained effort and concentration are required to maintain the forward setting.
- The arm muscles of a young beginner are under-developed.

18

MANIPULATION OF THE MOUTH APERTURE

The manipulations for speech are almost identical for those used for brass playing. Therefore a player has an established muscular memory of tongue and jaw movements to aid control of the mouth aperture.

Lower notes resonate more richly using an "open" vowel (natural cavity) and high notes resonate more sympathetically using "reduced" vowels (edge tones).

o (sounding "or") a e i
natural cavity . . . . edge tone

The mouth aperture resonances do not supply energy but act to regulate the flow of energy created by the breathing muscles.

Open vowel "o" sounding "or"

- This increases the aperture of the mouth by an extreme lowering of the jaw and causes the dorsum (rear) of the tongue to become concave. The lip aperture is also rounded.
  The acoustical effect is to reduce frictional vibration and increase the low overtones by allowing the air to resonate throughout the mouth aperture (natural cavity).
  When used in brass playing "o" produces a rich resonanace in the low register.

Medium vowel "a"

- This widens the mouth aperture by lowering the jaw and removing the sides of the tongue from the molars.
  The acoustical effect is to reduce frictional vibration and high overtones by enlarging the aperture within the mouth.
  When used in brass playing "a" produces a good resonance in the middle register.

Reduced vowels "i" and "e"

- These narrow the mouth aperture by raising the lower jaw and lifting the blades of the tongue towards the hard palate. These muscles also seal the sides of the tongue against the molars (edge tones).
  The acoustical effect is to accentuate frictional vibration and high overtones by reducing the aperture within the mouth.
  When used in brass playing "i" helps in the production of the highest notes, "e" for those notes slightly down in range.

Test the acoustical properties of these vowels by tapping your teeth with a pencil. By grading the tongue and jaw movements a recognizable melody can be produced. The natural aperture of the mouth is a major factor in determining how easily a player will achieve an extreme of range. A player with a large mouth aperture and a high roof to his mouth will resonate freely in the low register. This is because of the naturally low frictional qualities of his mouth aperture. High notes are often a problem to this player. They are achievable, but the muscles of the embouchure are placed under stress. The reverse is true for the player with a small mouth aperture. Teachers will be familiar with the immature trombonist or tuba player who reduces the frictional properties of his small mouth aperture by blowing out his cheeks. This is often the only way for a small child to resonate the low notes of these longer brass instruments. The size of the mouth aperture is therefore a matter for consideration when matching students to type of instrument.

Question 12	Answers	
Do you personally use the dorsum (rear) of your tongue to achieve range control?	Yes	60%
	Probably move the tongue a little	30%
	No	10%

Comment: For simplicity I shall refer to the trumpet and high horn players as the "upper end" and low horn players, baritone, trombonists and tuba players as the "lower end". Those instrumentalists that place most emphasis on the use of the dorsum of the tongue as a range controller are "upper end" players and those who are more casual about the use of the dorsum or who disclaim any use of it are mainly "lower end" players.

Question 13	Answers	
Do you encourage students to use the dorsum of their tongue to achieve range control?	Yes	52%
	Allow them to discover if for themselves	28%
	Might mention it in passing	10%
	No	10%

Comment: Again, it is the "upper end" player that encourages a student to use the dorsum of the tongue to help in range control. It would seem that all students, who have successfully mastered the "vowel" technique, achieve an easier top register without excessive mouthpiece weight, and a more resonant middle and lower register.

As in Question 11, the teachers of "lower end" instruments appear far more casual in the use of the tongue as a range controller.

Question 14	Answers	
Do you use a vertical jaw movement to achieve range control?	Yes, extensively	53%
	Yes, to some extent	29%
	No	18%

Comment: In answer to this question an interesting pattern begins to emerge. The responses of the "lower end" players became more positive whilst the "upper end" players put less emphasis on this aspect than on the use of the dorsum as a range controller.

Question 15	Answers	
If you use a vertical jaw movement, do you encourage a student to use a similar movement?	Yes	40%
	Allow them to discover it for themselves	23%
	No	22%
	Might mention it in passing	15%

Comment: "Lower end" players particularly stress this aspect of range control. These instrumentalists find that the student who can successfully master the vertical manipulation of the lower jaw achieve a security of note placing, and a resonance throughout the range.

Question 16	Answers	
Do you place any significance on the horizontal position of the lower jaw?	Yes	70%
	No	30%

Comment: To watch the players in performance was most revealing. Over 90% of my interviewees made a forward movement of the lower jaw from a masticating position to a biting position. Since the masticating position is a relaxed position each player had consciously decided to thrust the jaw forward or had found instinctively that they functioned best with the jaw in this position. This would explain the discrepancy between the verbal and practical response. As a further point of interest few players remained rigidly in the biting position.

Question 17	Answers	
If you place significance on this horizontal position do you encourage a student to establish any particular position?	Yes	55%
	Learning by observation	35%
	No	10%

Comment: Most players seem to guide their students towards the forward jaw position either by discussion or example. Reasons given for this preference were:

- To provide a secure structure for the lips
- To enhance lip flexibility

A fascinating point of interest which arises from Question 12 to Question 17 is the difference in emphasis between "upper end" and "lower end" groups of players regarding the tongue and jaw movements. There is a physiological explanation. The tongue and jaw share the function of regulating the mouth aperture but each has an individual use which befits a specific task.

The tongue has a complex muscular construction which makes it capable of the most subtle adjustments. This is particularly suitable for delicate manipulations between close harmonics towards the top of the register.

In the above examples both the trumpet player and the trombonist would use a combination of tongue and jaw manipulations. However, the trumpet player would sense a greater dependancy of the tongue while the trombonist would sense a balance between tongue and jaw.

The jaw manipulations are less subtle but provide greater stability for the embouchure. This makes it suitable for larger movements between widely spaced harmonics towards the bottom of the register.

In this example both the trumpet player and the trombonist would again use a combination of tongue and jaw manipulation. However, in this instance the trumpet player would sense a balance between tongue and jaw while the trombonist would sense a greater dependancy on the jaw manipulation. Variation in the degree of tongue and jaw movement depends on register. Consider the following:

- The highest note achievable on the piccolo trumpet requires a tongue manipulation to regulate the mouth aperture—the jaw being held in its highest position.
- The lowest note achievable on the double Bb tuba requires a jaw manipulation to regulate the mouth aperture—the tongue resting at the bottom of the mouth.

Within the above extremes are a multitude of co-ordinated manipulations between the tongue and jaw. The final positions selected depend upon the natural mouth aperture of the player, the instrument played and the notes required.

Another point of interest arises from Question 16. I have already stated that over 90% of my interviewees consciously or instinctively play with a forward movement of the jaw. Why? Because this setting is found to create a stable structure on which the embouchure muscles can perform by removing unwanted slack from the lower lip and flesh of the chin.

I think that it is a matter for concern if a teacher does not offer specific advice to a student on the setting of the lower jaw. In my experience, the majority of embouchure faults arise as a direct result of the jaw remaining in its passive position. The image of "shaving the chin" or "spreading lipstick on the lower lip" will often help to combine the forward jaw position with the desired texture of lip and chin.

As an alternative try the following:

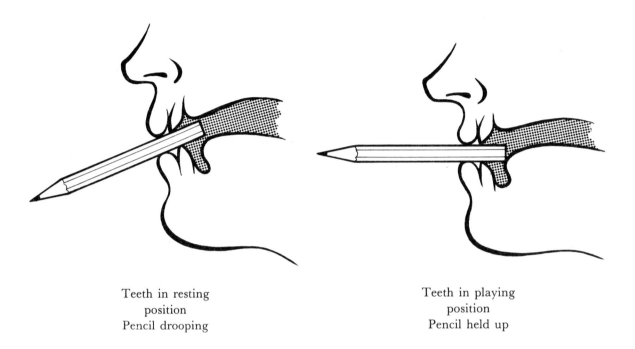

Teeth in resting
position
Pencil drooping

Teeth in playing
position
Pencil held up

It was apparent from performers that the forward jaw position once established was by no means inflexible. The horizontal position was constantly being adjusted in response to pitch. This does not mean that the jaw retreats to the passive masticating position for certain notes. It simply means that the jaw moves between certain personal parameters to provide the appropriate structure on which the lip tissue can most effectively function. It is found by most players that when tongue movement is combined with the vertical and horizontal jaw movements an easy flexibility is achieved.

The following diagrams show that the combination of vertical and horizontal movement causes the lower jaw to travel in a diagonal projection. This helps ease the embouchure into an appropriate position for the required notes. This will be discussed in detail in Chapter 5.

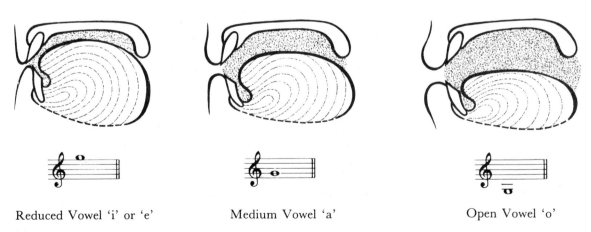

Reduced Vowel 'i' or 'e'

Medium Vowel 'a'

Open Vowel 'o'

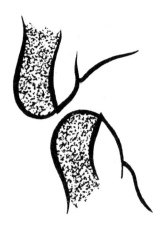

Standard Jaw Formation
The lower front teeth recede a small amount beneath the upper front teeth when the jaw is in its passive position.

Malformation 1 of the Jaw Formation
This is the most common deviation from the 'norm'. Recessive lower front teeth when the jaw is in its passive position.

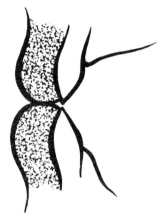

Malformation 2 of the Jaw Formation
This is unusual. The teeth bite and masticate in the same position. The muscles of the jaw are relaxed when the upper and lower front teeth are aligned.

Malformation 3 of the Jaw Formation
This is more unusual. The lower front teeth are set forward from the upper front teeth when the jaw muscles are relaxed.

IMPLICATIONS FOR PLAYERS WITH PHYSIOLOGICAL MALFORMATIONS OF THE LOWER JAW

As a general rule, these malformations cause little change in the vertical movement of the lower jaw. There are, however, considerable implications when considering horizontal movement.

Malformation 1. A player should experience few problems in achieving a standard horizontal jaw position. In general, I have noticed that a player with this malformation has a remarkable flexibility of the lower jaw muscles which allows forward movement of the lower teeth to establish a biting position. Sometimes a problem will occur when moving into the upper register. This is caused by too much recession of the lower teeth. The embouchure support is reduced allowing the chin muscles to become slack which makes it possible for the lower lip to slide upwards behind the top lip.

For high notes a player with **Malformation 1** should keep the lower and upper front teeth as near to alignment as is possible. A student may find it easier to think of holding his head in a slight downward position while raising the bell or mouthpiece. The effect, of course, is the same as keeping the jaw forwards.

23

Malformation 2. A player will not experience any problem in achieving the standard horizontal jaw position. The mouthpiece is merely placed on the embouchure with the lower jaw in its passive position, which in this instance is also the biting position. However, as a result of a very limited horizontal movement of the lower jaw, this player is unable to achieve the diagonal motion which helps in producing a flexible technique. Skilful use of the tongue can compensate for this deficiency.

Malformation 3. This jaw formation is generally accompanied by a short upper lip and an excessively fleshy, lower lip. It should be manipulated in opposite directions during horizontal movement.

To ascend
- The lower, front teeth must be pushed forward in order to tilt the instrument upwards.

To descend
- The lower, front teeth must be withdrawn in order to tilt the instrument downwards.

Such a player tends to attain greater success on the trumpet rather than on a lower brass instrument but seldom achieves a pleasing, warm sound.

DEVELOPMENT OF SENSITIVITY TO THE MOUTH APERTURE

Most of the functions of the mouth aperture are very familiar. However, some are of particular interest and benefit can be accrued by developing sensitivity to the manipulations involved.

- The mouth aperture is very nearly closed when:
  Sonding shhh!
  Hissing
- The mouth aperture is wide open when:
  Yawning
  Misting up glass with a breath
- The mouth aperture starts from very nearly closed and then opens when:
  Sucking through a straw
- The mouth aperture starts open and then closes when:
  Squirting liquid from a straw
- The mouth aperture alternatively opens and closes when:
  Chewing

FUNCTIONS OF THE MOUTH APERTURE IN RELATION TO BRASS PLAYING

These manipulations can be used to enhance range control on an instrument. Remember that in the musical examples given, there is an octave difference between the trumpet and trombone parts. Therefore there will be a corresponding difference in the physiological approach. The trumpet player will depend more heavily on the tongue movements while the trombonist will utilize more lower jaw movement.
- The mouth aperture is very nearly closed when playing high notes.

Trumpet   Trombone

- The mouth aperture is wide open when playing low notes.

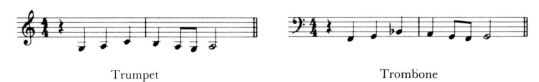

Trumpet   Trombone

24

- The mouth aperture starts from very nearly closed and then opens when moving from a high to a low note.

Trumpet   Trombone

- The mouth aperture starts open and very nearly closes when moving from a low to a high note.

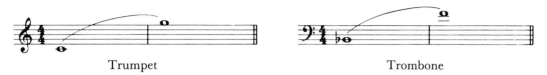

Trumpet   Trombone

- The mouth aperture alternatively opens and closes when moving from a low to a high note and back again.

Trumpet   Trombone

5 RESISTANCE AT THE LIP APERTURE, 'THE NOTE CONTROLLER'

The lip aperture works together with the breathing muscles in regulating the speed of lip vibration and, in so doing, establishes the general range within which the notes will most effectively sound. This aperture is the next area of subsidiary resistance after the breath has left the glottal aperture.

ANATOMICAL DESCRIPTION OF THE EMBOUCHURE MUSCLES WHICH CREATE THE LIP APERTURE:

Each embouchure muscle, with a single exception, is attached at one end to the skull. The other ends of these muscles meet at a point called the modiolus. The exception is the 'obicularis oris', the lip muscle, which is circular. This is not attached to the skull although it does meet the other muscles at the modiolus.

A muscle is constituted by overlapping fibres which connect to the brain nerves. The nerves carry electrical messages from the brain to each muscle about when to contract and by how much. This results in a shortening of the muscle concerned and a movement of the surrounding flesh.

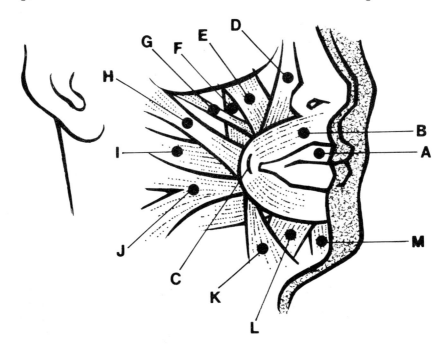

A The Red Membrane are the lips—they vibrate against the airstream.

B The Obicularis Oris is the circular muscle that surrounds the red membrane. In two portions, upper and lower. The obicularis oris brings the lips together.

C The Modiolus is where the obicularis oris and other face muscles meet at each side of the lips. The setting of the modiolus determines the width of the lip aperture.

D The Levator Nasi is joined at one end to the nose and at the other to the obicularis oris. The levator nasi raises the centre of the upper lip.

E The Levator Superioris is joined at one end to the eye bone and at the other to the obicularis oris. The levator superioris raises the bulk of the upper lip.

F The Levator Anguli Oris is joined at one end to the eye bone and at the other to the obicularis oris. The levator anguli oris raises the ends of the upper lip.

26

G The Zygomaticus Minor is joined at one end to the outside of the eye bone and at the other to the obicularis oris. The zygomaticus minor pulls the outer ends of the upper lip towards the temples.

H The zygomaticus major is joined at one end to the cheek bone and at the other to the obicularis oris. The Zygomaticus Major pulls the corners of the lips towards the cheek bone.

I The Buccinator is joined at one end to the lower cheek bone and at the other to the obicularis oris. The buccinator pulls the corners of the lips towards the ears.

J The Risorius divides and is joined at one end to two separate parts of the jaw bone and at the other the obicularis oris. The risorius pulls the corners of the lips towards the jaw bone.

K The Depressor Anguli Oris is joined at one end to the chin and at the other to the obicularis oris. The depressor anguli pulls the corners of the lips towards the chin.

L The Depressor Inferioris is joined at one end to the outer edge of the chin bone and at the other to the obicularis oris. The depressor inferioris lowers the bulk of the lower lip.

M The Mentalis is joined at one end to the point of the chin and at the other to the obicularis oris. The mentalis pulls the centre of the lower lip towards the point of the chin.

The obicularis oris, the circular muscle, is the only face muscle that contracts inwards towards the centre of the lips. This contraction alone causes the lip aperture to shut so tightly as to prevent any penetration by the air stream.

The remaining facial muscles contract and shorten. These contractions alone pull the surrounding flesh away from the lips. This causes the lip aperture to open too wide for the lips to vibrate against the air stream.

The obicularis oris and the remaining facial muscles, when contracting at the same time, create a state of antagonistic contraction and cause the red membrane to become taut. This tension partially resists exhalation and in so doing results in an oscillation of the red membrane. A sound is produced.

The pitch of the note is determined by the speed of the oscillation. This speed is controlled by the degree of tension in the red membrane, the size of the lip aperture, and the breath pressure which is generated by the antagonistic contraction of the breathing muscles, the glottal aperture and the mouth aperture.

MANIPULATIONS OF THE LIP APERTURE:

The manipulations of the individual muscles that together control the shape of the aperture are also used to form a variety of facial expressions.

A student should study each of the following photographs and use a mirror to form a similar expression. This way the separate contractions are isolated and can then be combined to form the lip aperture.

■ Make a petulant facial expression. Feel the obicularis oris contracting inwards. This closes the lips.

■ Make a sneering facial expression. Feel the levator nasi, levator superioris and levator anguli oris contracting upwards. This raises and shortens the top lip.

■ Make an amused facial expression. Feel the zygomaticus, buccinator and risorios contracting outward. This shortens the cheeks.

■ Make a prim facial expression. Feel the angularis, depressor and mentalis contracting downwards. This shortens the bottom lip.

■ Make a determined facial expression. Feel the meeting point of the muscles ('the modiolus'). This 'sets' the embouchure and determines the width of the aperture.

■ Repeat the determined facial expression and part the teeth. Feel the formation of the lip aperture. This allows the red membrane to vibrate freely against the column of air.

The following questions cover a wide range of issues relating to breath resistance at the lip aperture. Because of this I will comment on each issue as it arises.

Question 18	Answers	
Do you give a student information on how the face muscles control the lip aperture?	Yes, in detail	20%
	Yes, in general terms	40%
	No	40%

Comment: You will observe that there exists a clear division of opinion. Each reply appeared to relate directly to the teacher's learning experience. The teacher whose learning process had been largely instinctive and free from obvious embouchure problems considered it unnecessary to develop an awareness of the physiology. On the other hand, the teacher who had become skilled through systematic instruction or conversely had experienced real playing problems through haphazard instruction tended to be more analytical in his teaching. However, there was general agreement that a player thinks about music and not about physiology when performing.

Another factor to emerge was that tuba players in particular adopted a more casual attitude towards embouchure matters. A probable reason for this is the size of mouthpiece which tolerates greater embouchure irregularities than that of the trumpet.

Having experienced the unsatisfactory nature of haphazard teaching, I have attempted to establish a more systematic approach.

- Teach the skills and develop an understanding of anatomy until the manipulations and information are recorded in muscular memory.
- Check daily, during practice, to ensure against muscular abuse.
- Focus on the music during performance and not on the physiology.

I have found that the long term benefits from this approach to playing are far reaching:

- The performer who has a genuine knowledge of anatomy and an understanding of the way in which this relates to brass playing is able and confident to make adjustments to the embouchure as the need occurs. This reduces stress.
- The performer who has a genuine knowledge of anatomy becomes a more sensitive and effective teacher.

Question 19	Answers	
Do you prefer a student to play with a specific embouchure formation?	Yes	45%
	Reject a student with a weak embouchure	28%
	No	27%

Comment: A teacher's attitude would appear to be formed by his learning experience and working environment. Those teachers answering 'No', are invariably instinctive players who received little or no guidance on physiological matters during their formative years of playing. They are firmly of the opinion that a student will find the embouchure that is most suitable to his physiology and purpose.

The 28% who reject students with poorly formed embouchures are instrumentalists teaching at conservetoire or university. Members of this group consider that a student who has failed to achieve a sound physiological approach by the time of entry audition is unsuited to a professional course.

Those who answered 'Yes', transverse all categories. Some are teachers who have developed their skills instinctively but are determined that their students should benefit from a more analytical and systematic approach to learning. Others became skilful as a result of receiving methodical instruction and have adopted a similar approach themselves. However, the majority of those who replied 'Yes', are the teachers of younger students and beginners. As a group these tend to be more fastidious in establishing a good physical approach.

In my opinion it is helpful if the teacher has a definite mental image of a good embouchure. This gives the teacher confidence to offer positive instruction when a student is in need of support. However, the image should not be so clearly defined that it excludes the possibility of flexibility.

The variety of bone structure, jaw formation, teeth formation, teeth length, lip texture, lip length and the natural 'set' of the facial expression makes as many different embouchures as there are faces. For instance most strong embouchures appear to 'nip' down at the corners of the mouth. However, in some cases, the mouth turns up naturally at the corners giving the appearance of an exaggerated smile when the modiolus is set. The teacher must judge whether the cheek muscles are pulling too strongly or whether this exaggerated smile is as a result of the natural facial expression.

Nevertheless, the brass player has a definitely recognizable facial expression. Some call it aggressive. This is due to the growth of certain muscles of the face and is caused by the continual antagonistic activity of the upward, outward, downward and inward contractions. Most evidence of muscular development is found both over the top lip and to a lesser extent under the bottom lip (the upper and lower part of the obicularis oris) and at the sides of the mouth (the modiolus) where most of the muscles meet.

Before moving onto the next question I should like to discuss the difference between the instinctive player and the player who requires a reasoned process in order to develop his skill. The definition of instinct is intuition which in turn is defined as an immediate mental apprehension without reasoning. In my opinion, this perfectly describes the instinctive player. These students are particularly observant and can apprehend merely by watching another embouchure at work. Others who do not possess the same visual sensibility but who are equally musical can achieve the same result. This may take longer to accomplish but if the embouchure is established through a reasoned process the muscular memory rarely fails.

Question 20	Answers
How do you create the image of an embouchure in the mind of a student?	Observing the teacher's embouchure 55% Using an appropriate analogy 40% Studying photographs of the embouchures of established players 5%

Comment: I find each of these ideas to be most useful and suggest that they be incorporated within a lesson using the following order of presentation:

- Information on the anatomy. This provides theoretical appreciation of each muscular function.
- Exercises to manipulate the individual muscles based on facial expressions. This provides a practical appreciation of each muscular function.
- An appropriate analogy. This provides a theoretical appreciation of the working of groups of muscles in antagonistic contraction.
- Photographs of established players and a suggestion to observe the teacher's embouchure as it functions. This reinforces the understanding of antagonistic contraction.
- A mirror. It is important that regular visual checks are made during the early stages of forming an embouchure or during remedial work. Repetition of the correct muscular co-ordination soon establishes the correct muscular memory. When this happens the student is able to become less dependant on the mirror and depend more on the 'feel' of the embouchure.

Question 21

If you use an analogy to help explain the formation of the embouchure, what is it?

Approximately one third of the interviewees who use analogies to help establish a beginner's embouchure suggest the following:

Try to hold your mouth in a position half way between a smile and a whistle.

This analogy is generally accepted to be a useful and concise way of introducing a complex concept. It encourages the outward contraction of the muscles in the cheeks (the smile) to work in antagonistic contraction against the compression muscles, (the whistle).

The following is an abbreviated quote from Farkas. I recommend that a student should take the trouble to read the whole analogy.

We shall start with a coffee can, without a lid . . . . This can will represent the brass player's skull. Next we procure a cloth bag, similar to a marble-bag. . . . with a drawstring run through it. The bag will now represent the entire covering of the skull. Of course, the drawstring-controlled opening in the bag is going to represent the player's mouth.

Philip Farkas, The Art of Brass Playing. Pub. Wind Music Inc.

I use the following analogy:

EMBOUCHURE
('CHOPS')

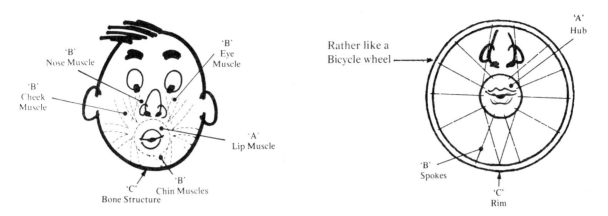

A) Lip Muscle/Hub — Hold firm with corners locked in position.

B) Cheek, Chin, Eye & Nose Muscles/Spokes — Pull away from the lip muscle and join the bone structure.

C) Bone Structure/Rim — To which the spokes are attached.

The Spokes have to be tightened equally —

(Ask your teacher to help you look like 'GREAT CHOPS')

'GREAT-CHOPS'

Otherwise Your Wheel Will Buckle

'BUNCH-CHOPS'   'SMILEY-CHOPS'   'PUFFER-CHOPS'   'DROOPY-CHOPS'

John Ridgeon, 'New Horizons for the Young Brass Player'. Brasswind Pub.

Question 22	Answers
What advice do you offer to a student who finds difficulty in forming a lip aperture?	1. Use the air column to open the lip aperture. 2. Separate the teeth. 3. Place the tip of a pencil between the lips. Set the embouchure muscles around the pencil. Freeze the muscles and remove the pencil. Blow air through remaining hole until resistance to the air column is sufficient to excite the red membrane to vibrate.

Comment: The majority of my interviewees encourage their students to sense the air column opening the lip aperture. Students who utilize minimum mouthpiece pressure possess the lip sensitivity to respond to the advice. Those students who utilize too much mouthpiece pressure numb the red membrane which causes insensitivity to the air column as it passes through the lips. Those instrumentalists are unable to respond to the sensory stimulation and therefore rely too literally on the wording of this advice. This often causes the lips to vibrate against each other rather than against the air column as intended, resulting in a 'slapping' effect. This makes:

- An uncontrollable crackle in the tone
- or, a thin unattractive tone
- or back pressure of the air column.

Separating the teeth can be the simplest way of creating a lip aperture but again success depends upon the physical sensitivity of the student. An exaggerated opening of the teeth can cause the mouthpiece to 'set-in' the lower lip resulting in:

- A lip aperture which is inflexible
- A lip aperture which is too widely spread and/or, poor stamina.

The pencil technique is most appropriately used by a beginner or a student who has experienced an embouchure breakdown or a student who lacks in lip sensitivity. This approach combines visual and tactile stimulation and the best results are achieved by cross checking a mirror image of the aperture against a photograph of a well formed aperture.

It is essential that a student should understand the role of the lip aperture as a note controller. The red membrane vibrates in resistance to exhalation and consequently:

- The smaller the lip aperture, the greater the resistance, the higher the note.
- The larger the lip aperture, the lesser the resistance, the lower the note.

I approach the formation of the lip aperture with students of all ages as follows:

- Study the sketches which show how the muscles co-ordinate to form the lip aperture. Notice how the musculature bears a striking resemblance to a bicycle wheel.

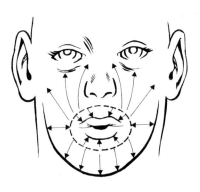  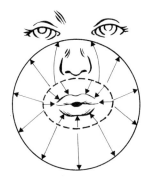

The lip muscle (or hub) is the centre of the embouchure and by contracting inwards, tries to close the lip aperture.

The cheek, chin, eye and nose muscles (or spokes) are joined to the lip muscle and the bone structure. When they contract, they shorten and in so doing pull the lips apart.

The bone structure (or rim) is the framework to which one end of each outward contracting muscle is attached.

■ Practice isolating the contraction of each individual muscle. Imitate the facial expressions on page 27 and 28.

■ Attempt to co-ordinate the contractions. The face should look like this:

■ Separate the red membrane in the centre of the lips. This can be practised by blowing through a straw which accomplishes:

The contraction of the lip muscle as the lips close to hold the straw.

The contraction of the nose, eye, cheek and chin muscles as they attempt to stop the lips from squashing the straw.

The set of the modiolus as the two sets of opposing muscles balance.

The free flow of air through the lip aperture.

The straw acts as a crutch for the muscles by artificially holding the lips apart.

■ Maintain the lip aperture and therefore the free flow of air when the crutch is removed.

Shorten the centre of the top lip by contracting the nose muscles. See sneering facial expression on page 27 or think of a nasty smell.

Shorten the centre of the bottom lip by contracting the chin muscles. See prim facial expression on page 28, or think of the chin position for shaving, or think of putting on lip-stick.

Set the balance of the opposing muscles. See the determined expression on page 28 or place both little fingers in the mouth corners and say 'p'.

Note the 'diamond' shape when this is achieved.

In my experience, the student who forms his lip aperture in the above manner develops manipulative sensitivity and a sound knowledge of the embouchure.

6 VARIATION OF RESISTANCE AT THE LIP APERTURE

In Chapter 5, I concentrated on the physiology of the face, the co-ordination of the musculature and the formation of the lip aperture. In this chapter I aim to explore the way in which the brass player varies the resistance to the air column by changing the lip aperture.

It is necessary to start by considering the 'set' of the modiolus. You will recollect that the modiolus is not a muscle but the meeting points of the opposing face muscles occurring on either side of the lips.

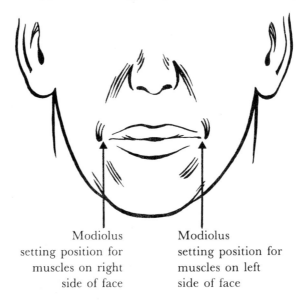

Modiolus
setting position for
muscles on right
side of face

Modiolus
setting position for
muscles on left
side of face

The points at which the modiolus are 'set' control the texture of the lips.

- Set nearer the centre, the lips become fleshy and produce a warm, full tone suitable for the trombone or tuba.
- Set further away from the centre, the lips become thinner and produce a bright tone suitable for the trumpet.

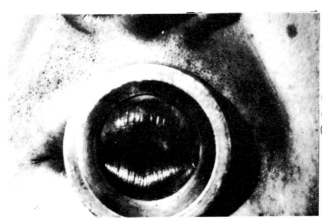

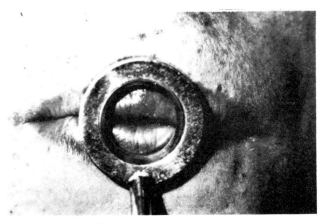

Trombone setting

Trumpet setting

Once the lip texture has been selected to suit the instrument played, the anatomy and the required tone, the modiolus 'setting' remains unchanged regardless of the pitch of the note. **The notion that the lips are stretched for high notes and slackened for low notes is exceedingly dangerous. This results in a thin tone at the top and a woolly tone at the bottom.**

TO CHANGE PITCH THE FOLLOWING METHOD SHOULD BE ADOPTED:

- **High Notes**: Apply more effort towards inward and outward muscle contractions. This results in the lip aperture becoming smaller, without closing, and the surrounding tissue becoming firmer. A greater resistance to the air column is achieved and results in a higher note.
- **Low Notes**: Apply less effort towards inward muscle contractions so that the required malleability of tissue is achieved and the lip aperture is increased. This reduces resistance to the air column and results in a lower note.
- Try playing a **low** note followed by a **high** note in front of a mirror. At a cursory glance, it may appear that the corners pull back for high notes and set closer for low notes. This is not the case. The cursory glance will be attracted by the more obvious movement associated with the outward contraction of the cheek muscles. The less obvious, inward contraction of the lip muscle may escape attention.

  Look again, but concentrate the gaze at the lip corners, just beside the mouthpiece rim. These also appear to move away from the two centres of antagonistic contraction, but in this instance, the movement is inward towards the lip aperture.

  Confirm that the 'tug-of-war' is balanced by placing your index finger on the outside of the modiolus. Play again the low note followed by the high note. You should clearly feel the cheek muscles contracting outwards from the meeting points, the modiolus.

Cheek muscles contracting outwards from the modiolus

Now place your finger on the inside of the modiolus. Play again the low note followed by the high note. You should clearly feel the lip muscles contracting from the meeting points, the modiolus, inwards towards the lip aperture.

Lip muscles contracting inwards from the modiolus

35

Having discovered the appropriate setting point of the modiolus, we are now unable to explore how the musculature works around this anchor in order to control note selection.

Question 23	Answers
How do your students develop lip sensitivity? (I define lip sensitivity as the ability to perceive when the lip tissue responds properly to a defined simulation and the ability to be able to repeat that response on demand.)	Through the performing of lip flexibility exercises. Through the removal of excessive mouthpiece pressure. Through buzzing.

Comment: I have listed the three principle ways in which my interviewees encourage their students to develop lip sensitivity. It would have been erroneous to have listed the answers as percentages since most replies mentioned a combination of the above means. For simplicity, I intend to deal with each point separately but ask you to remember that the first answer was rarely mentioned without reference to the second.

LIP FLEXIBILITY EXERCISES

These must contain certain features in order to develop a heightened sensitivity to the lip aperture. The features are:

- Simplicity of fingering or slide technique so that the mind can be concentrated on the manipulations of the lip aperture and the supporting embouchure muscles. This is less essential as the skills become more advanced.
- The harmonic series should be so arranged as to require a largish and therefore instantly recognisable lip movement. This becomes less essential as the skills become more advanced.
- The demands should become more subtle and complex as sensitivity increases.
- The exercises should be constructed in such a way as to make execution impossible if excessive mouthpiece pressure is applied.
- The exercises should be repetitious so that the player, having once sensed the correct lip movement, can consolidate the technique.

When playing the above, a student should sense:

LOW C: The lip muscle (obicularis oris) thickens the membrane as if for a low note whistle.

The outward contracting muscle balance the lip muscles and in so-doing control the cheeks and chin but allow malleability.

The 'set' of the modiolus remains unchanged.

Remember to help the embouchure muscles by using minimum mouthpiece pressure, lowering the back of the tongue, and opening the teeth.

THIRD SPACE C: The lip muscle (obicularis oris) thins the membrane as if for a high note whistle.

The outward contracting muscles balance the lip muscle and in so doing control the cheeks and chin, resulting in a firm appearance.

The 'set' of the modiolus remains unchanged.

Remember to help the embouchure muscles by using marginally more mouthpiece pressure to ensure an airtight seal, raising the back of the tongue, and raising the lower teeth. It will also help if the speed of the breath is increased.

G: The lip muscle (obicularis oris) forms a membrane texture somewhere between the two Cs.

The outward contracting muscles balance the lip muscle and in so doing control the cheeks and chin and result in a texture a somewhere between malleable and firm.

The 'set' of the modiolus remains unchanged.

Remember to help the embouchure muscles by appropriately adjusting the mouthpiece pressure, the back of the tongue, the jaw and the speed of exhalation.

In this exercise the 'G' is approached in contrasting ways. When the movement to 'G' is approached from low 'C' and returns to low 'C', then the 'G' becomes a clearly defined focal point. For a brief moment, the musculature freezes the lip aperture and texture. The same applies when the 'G' is sandwiched between the 3rd space 'C' 's. But, when the 'G' is slipped in between the low 'C' and the 3rd space 'C', the musculature does not freeze. In this instance, the player has to sense the membrane 'clipping' the harmonic. When true lip sensitivity is achieved these passing harmonics can be 'focused' as clearly as the more defined harmonics.

The exercise below is designed to help more advanced players develop sensitivity to these passing harmonics.

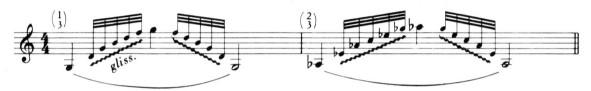

I agree with my interviewees who claim that the regular practice of lip flexibilities can enhance lip sensitivity. However, unless this is approached with due care and consideration more harm than good can result.

REMOVAL OF EXCESSIVE MOUTHPIECE PRESSURE:

Excessive mouthpiece pressure is definitely one of the most serious faults the horn player can have. It makes his playing sound laboured, reduces flexibility, hardens the tone and decreases endurance by at least half.

Philip Farkas, *The Art of French Horn Playing*. Summy Birchard Music Copyright © 1956 Birch Tree Group Ltd.
Used by permission.

It is unrealistic to expect a student who has numbed his lips through excessive mouthpiece pressure to play in a responsive and sensitive way. Pressure desensitizes the lips so that the player becomes unaware as to the degree of pressure being applied. The quote from Farkas spells out the principle ramifications of excessive pressure but if a student requires other warning signals a mirror will help. Look for:

- Blanched little finger in hook.
- Third finger hooked around the third valve.
- The whole of the palm of the holding hand pressed hard against the instrument.
- Arms tight against the sides of the chest.
- Tension in the neck muscles.
- Severe indentation of the lips.
- Scar tissue on the inside of the red membrane.

Pressure first occurs at the beginner stage. Hands are held tight with excitement and through the desire to hold the instrument securely. Pressure can also occur when a note is produced too high too soon. In the case of a beginner trumpet player, a 'G' second line can cause this problem. As 'G' is a very common note to start on, and as the majority achieve this note most readily, I had better explain my misgivings.

Very few beginner trumpet players have the necessary strength of embouchure muscle to play 'G' without some artificial 'crutch'. To prove this ask a beginner to 'buzz' the note without the support of the mouthpiece. The result will be a very poor 'buzz' with the lips 'slapping' hard against each other, or alternatively a noticeably lower 'buzz'.

In order to achieve the 'G', a beginner trumpet player has to support his underdeveloped lip muscles with his arm muscles. By applying mouthpiece pressure to the lips the length of vibrating tissue is reduced, which has the same effect as placing a finger on a vibrating violin string. The mouthpiece pressure also firms and flattens the lip tissue. This flattened embouchure makes higher notes available by reducing the dimensions of the aperture which in turn offers greater resistance to the breath exhalation.

The instant rewards of excessive pressure are short lived. The blood, and therefore the oxygen, is prevented from fuelling the lip muscle, which causes fatigue and, in the longer term, stunts muscle growth.

My approach to the beginner is to allow the inevitable 'G' but to point out the pressure involved. When the note is repeated, I encourage the removal of tension in the arms and hands and the note gradually sinks to 'C'. At this point, I beam approval, and the pupil learns to associate success with relaxation. This is possibly the most important lesson to be learnt at the beginner stage.

As the player progresses, pressure can also develop through:

- the development of the high register
- fatigue
- nervous tension

Harmful accumulation of excessive mouthpiece pressure can be avoided by diligent practice. Never use pressure when the embouchure muscles are fresh. Never use pressure for low notes. Never grip the instrument.

It would be wrong to assume that I subscribe to the doctrine of "non-pressure playing". On the contrary, I would describe my stance as positively in favour of *controlled* pressure rather than reluctantly accepting its inevitability.

I will enlarge on this to avoid any confusion. The embouchure muscles are capable of considerable development and will, if trained properly, play high notes with very little pressure. However, there comes a point where the tone becomes thin and eventually no further range can be added. The thinness of tone is created by the lack of seal between embouchure and mouthpiece. This is not a problem in the low register where the lips are malleable and are therefore capable of cushioning the mouthpiece. However, for high notes, where the lips become firmer and rounder in shape, the flat mouthpiece fails to 'bed' properly. This results in an air leak and a thin sound.

Each individual is limited in range by the character of his musculature and other physical characteristics. Nevertheless it is quite astonishing how much additional range can be added to the player's natural ceiling by the application of a *little* judicious mouthpiece pressure. Two important factors have to be borne in mind before following this advice.

- Pressure is only safe when applied to a strong and sound embouchure.
- Pressure should be judiciously removed for low note playing.

A similar situation exists in relation to fatigue. Every player uses more pressure when the muscles are tired. There is no harm in this. Go ahead and use it as a crutch but make sure that you remove this crutch when not required. Remember, the danger is from the insensitivity that develops through constant, excessive pressure.

BUZZING:

When a good buzz is forthcoming, put the mouthpiece, on its own, to the lips and without pressure continue to buzz through the mouthpiece. As soon as a good tone comes, try to hold onto it but do not press the mouthpiece to the lips as they must be free to buzz and vibrate.

Barry Tuckwell, Playing the Horn. OUP

A total of 98% of my interviewees use the buzz for one purpose or another.

Regularly with a mouthpiece or visualizer	60%
Extensively without a mouthpiece or visualizer	28%
Sometimes with a mouthpiece or visualizer	5%
Sometimes without a mouthpiece or visualizer	5%

Not all, however, agreed that it had any special qualities as a sensitisor of the red membrane. Other reasons given for buzzing were to loosen the lips at the beginning of the day, to strengthen the lip muscles and to help in developing a beginner's embouchure

Buzzing correctly causes the modiolus point to be selected according to the instrument played, or to be played. This establishes the texture of the red membrane. The muscular contraction of the levator nasi (nose muscles) and the depressers (chin muscles) are exaggerated a little so that between them the following shape of lip aperture and embouchure is created.

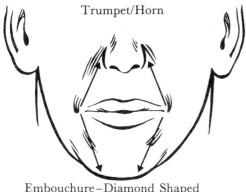

Trumpet/Horn

Embouchure–Diamond Shaped
Aperture Size–Oboe Reed

Trombone/Tuba

Embouchure–Diamond Shaped
Aperture Size–Bassoon Reed.

A gap between the teeth is opened to suit the instrument played, or to be played, and a note is selected to be 'buzzed'. This note should 'sit' towards the lower range of the instrument. This is most important. It serves no useful purpose for a trombonist to attempt to 'buzz' in the trumpet register. Having established the texture of the lip, and the shape of the embouchure and lip aperture, a column of air is made to penetrate the hole. As it does so, the red membrane surrounding it vibrates. **The resulting noise should be a free and easy sound with a distinguishable pitch.**

Buzzing incorrectly causes the modiolus to be set in an exaggerated smile. The lips are pressed together by the obicularis oris (lip muscle), and the lower jaw is too close to the top teeth and, more likely too far back towards the chewing position. **The resulting noise is more like a squeak than a buzz.** This creates a weak and vulnerable embouchure. The air column is also prevented from passing through the lip aperture. This doubles back on itself and causes head and throat pressure.

Equally incorrect is when the modiolus is set in an exaggerated 'puckered' position and the lips are bunched. **The resulting noise is now more like a 'raspberry'.** The embouchure lacks any vestige of controlled tension and is incapable of producing high notes.

However, if these rather obvious faults are avoided, the buzz can be one way of making the student aware of that unseen part of the embouchure that resides inside the mouthpiece cup. This is just as beneficial to the mature player as it is to the beginner. Try sensing the following:

- The red membrane vibrating against the air and not lip against lip.
- The roundish nature of the lip aperture, and not a crack.
- The large lip aperture for the low buzz.
- The smaller lip aperture for the high buzz.

- The slower lip vibration for the low buzz.
- The quicker lip vibration for the high buzz.
- The thickness of the lip tissue for the low buzz.
- The thinner lip tissue for the high buzz.
- The distance between the teeth when the lip aperture buzzes low.
- The closeness of the teeth when the lip aperture buzzes high.

By this means the student can begin to develop sensitivity to the resisting nature of the lip aperture and a genuine understanding of the part played by the buzz. The following is a useful last test:

- Moisten the back of one's hand and place it approximately four inches in front of the buzz. Sense the nature and direction of the air column. If the lower jaw is correctly positioned, the air column will penetrate at right angles to the face and flow freely in a broad channel. If the lower jaw is in its passive position and the lip aperture is a crack, the air column will penetrate in a chinward direction and be diffused over a wide area. If this latter situation occurs, a number of aspects are wrong, and, as a result, the buzz will be doing more harm than good.

When the 'buzz' is correct, 'buzz' into the mouthpiece. The student should sense a slight change (refer back to the Tuckwell quote). This change is caused by the embouchure muscles accommodating the presence of the mouthpiece, and is essential in order to seal the two surfaces, one being rounded, the other being flat. The student will also hear that the buzz/note will rise in pitch. This is caused by the presence of the mouthpiece rim which shortens the area of vibrating lip and results in a faster vibration.

Test this by buzzing without the mouthpiece and touch the buzz just where a trumpet or horn mouthpiece would make contact. The pitch will rise. The closer the touch to the lip aperture the higher the resulting buzz. This explains why some high note players, and players with weak embouchures, choose to play on a small diameter mouthpiece. This experiment is less successful for trombonists or tuba players.

When buzzing on the mouthpiece, the student should attempt to make a warm rounded buzz/note. If the sound is like a crackle, it will be because the aperture has collapsed. This problem can be resolved with the mouthpiece in place. First, position the mouthpiece and seal the edges. Then, as the buzz/note occurs, gradually open the aperture by raising the nose muscles, lowering the chin muscles and holding the modiolus in the 'set' position. This is a valuable exercise. The student is able to hear a significant change in the tone quality as the characteristic aperture shape is created.

A common fault, which occurs when establishing contact with the mouthpiece, is to raise the top lip and trap the lips apart with the rim. This is a clear sign of the player who uses too much pressure and has little or no muscle flexibility.

You will have realised that I am a regular user of the 'buzz' when developing a new embouchure and when sensitizing the more experienced player to the functions of the lip aperture. Nevertheless, a word of warning. Some students find it difficult to 'buzz'. In such cases, the teacher should endeavour not to treat the situation as a challenge to their prowess as a 'buzz' producer. It can result in the student developing a mental block. In preference move directly on to playing on the mouthpiece or instrument. Faults that occur can be rectified by the judicious use of a probing finger and by ensuring that the student is aware of the tone changing with the embouchure adjustment.

In addition to the three suggestions listed by my interviewees I recommend two further methods of developing lip sensitivity:

- The half buzz scale without fingering or slide change. This is only suitable for experienced players.
- Whistling. This is suitable for beginners and experienced players alike.

I find it advantageous to prepare a student by developing a general sensitivity to different parts of the body. This enables a player to remove all unnecessary tension and in this way conserves energy, prolonging the period before fatigue becomes apparent. So:

- Hang the hands loosely by the sides and sense the blood pulsing through the fingers.
- Sense the heart working. Attempt to control the beat rate.

- Waggle the ears and scalp.
- Twitch the nose . . . .

THE HALF BUZZ SCALE WOTHOUT FINGERING OR SLIDE CHANGE

This is helpful in reducing mouthpiece pressure and adjusting the relationship between upper lip and upper teeth.

Buzz a 'G' (second line) for trumpet. Buzz an 'F' (fourth line) for trombone. Continue to buzz whilst placing the mouthpiece in light contact with the lips. The embouchure should make no adjustment to seal the mouthpiece to the lips. In the absence of a seal, much of the air escapes, resulting in a half note/half buzz. Contract the embouchure muscles progressively, and support with the other areas of resistance. **Do not add mouthpiece pressure.**

By this means it is possible to complete a scale without using valves or a slide. The harmonic series has a less dominating influence because half the buzz occurs outside the instrument. The value of this exercise lies in the player's struggle to establish notes against the natural focusing of the harmonic series. It is impossible to achieve this without being acutely conscious of the minute adjustments of the lip aperture.

The pressure player learns to rely more on his embouchure muscles, in addition to increasing lip aperture sensitivity. The player with a poor upper lip/upper teeth relationship learns to align the two more effectively, in addition to increasing lip aperture sensitivity.

THE WHISTLE:

This is helpful in encouraging beginners and more experienced players to co-ordinate the lip aperture movements with the other resisters.

- Whistle a low note:
  The lip aperture is large
  The lip texture is thick
  The tongue is low in the mouth
  The jaw is held low
  The breath is exhaled slowly
- Whistle a high note:
  The lip aperture is small
  The lip texture is thinner
  The tongue is higher in the mouth
  The jaw is slightly higher
  The breath travels faster
- Whistle any note softly followed by a loud whistle on the same note:
  The lip aperture is larger for the loud note

This demonstrates the interdependence of the resisters. As the breath and the glottal resistance is reduced for the loud whistle, the air passes from the lip aperture at a faster speed. This would normally result in a sharpening of the note, but when the lip aperture compensates for this extra friction by enlarging, the original pitch is maintained. The reverse is, of course, true for the diminuendo.

The value of this exercise is in the opportunity to co-ordinate the lip aperture movements with the other resisters without the encumbrance of the mouthpiece. The beginner has the chance to experience the correct sensations before committing them to muscular memory. The experienced player has the chance to experience the correct sensations before returning to the instrument. Remedial work is best commenced in isolation from familiar sensations. The presence of the mouthpiece is sufficient to 'trigger' old habits.

Question 24	Answers
How do you advise your students to vary breath resistance at the lips in relation to note control?	By adjusting the size of the lip aperture 60%
	By observing a good example 25%
	By finding their own solution 15%

Comment: Most of my interviewees agree that resistance of the breath is varied at the lips by adjusting the size of the lip aperture. To reiterate, this is made possible by three factors:

- The lip muscle contracting inwards, towards the centre of the red membrane, and closing the lips.
- The remaining three groups of face muscles contracting outwards, away from the centre of the red membrane, and opening the lips.
    The levator muscles lift the top lip.
    The depressor muscles pull down the lower lip.
    The cheek muscles pull out the corners of the lips.
- The modiolus being 'set' by the balanced antagonistic contraction of the above muscles. The modiolus 'set' determines the texture of the red membrane for a specific instrument. Once the modiolus position is established it stays in place regardless of the low/high adjustment of the lip aperture.

Subtle control of the lip aperture is made possible by interrelationships of the three factors. Study the following:

Low Notes

Features

1. Large aperture with malleable lip tissue and thick, red membrane.
2. Long lips with the flesh, surrounding the nose, and the flesh, surrounding the chin, made malleable.
3. Face tissue is malleable.
4. 'Set' of the modiolus is less obvious.

Approach

1. Slacken, without relaxing, the lip muscle. Gently contract the lips into a shape suitable for a low whistle.
2. Slacken the nose and eye muscles to lengthen the upper lip and to make the flesh, surrounding the nose, malleable. Slacken the chin muscles to lengthen the lower lip and to make the flesh, covering the chin, malleable.
3. Slacken the cheek muscles.
4. A less forceful balanced contraction of the lip, nose, eye, cheek and chin muscles.

Reasons

1. A large aperture, thick red membrane and malleable lip tissue offer less breath resistance and result in a slow lip vibration.
2. The lips are long because the teeth are further apart, therefore requiring more flesh to cover the structure. The flesh is malleable because the muscles beneath are working less.
3. Malleable face tissue gives the lip muscle an opportunity to slacken and create a malleable lip tissue.
4. The 'set' of the modiolus is less obvious because the facial muscles have slackened in contraction.

42

High Notes

Features

1. Small aperture with firm lip tissue and thin red membrane
2. Short lips with flesh surrounding chin and flesh surrounding nose held firm.
3. Face tissue is firm.
4. 'Set'of the modiolus is obvious.

Approach

1. Contract the lip muscle towards the centre of the red membrane in a circular fashion and hold the red membrane onto the supporting teeth.
2. Contract the nose and eye muscles to shorten the upper lip and to make the flesh, surrounding the nose, firm. Contract the chin muscles to shorten the lower lip and to make the flesh, covering the chin, firm.
3. Contract the cheek muscles.
4. Balance the contractions of lip, nose, eye, cheek and chin muscles.

Reasons

1. A small aperture, thin red membrane and firm lip tissue offer great breath resistance and result in fast lip vibration.
2. The lips are short because the teeth are close together, therefore requiring little flesh to cover the structure.
3. Firm face muscles give the lip muscle an opportunity to contract firmly and create a firm lip tissue.
4. The 'set' of the modiolus is obvious because all the facial muscles are contracting.

TRANSITION FROM ONE SETTING TO ANOTHER

The task of setting a good looking and sounding embouchure for a defined note is not difficult. The problem occurs when moving from one 'setting' to another:

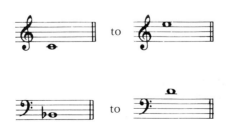

The following frames show a balanced transition:

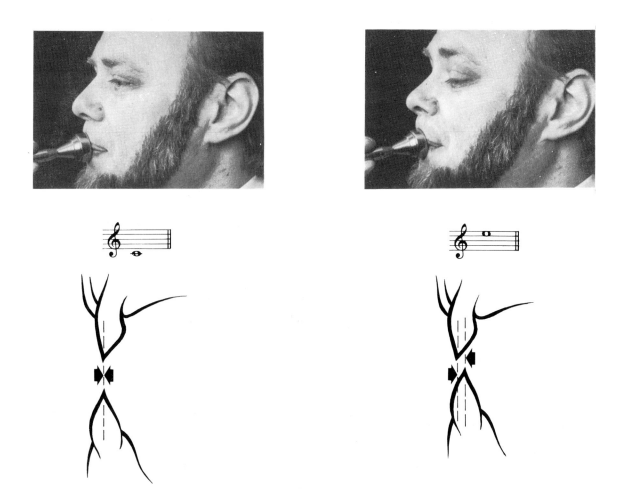

Notice:

- The modiolus setting remains unchanged but is more defined for high notes than for low notes.
- The lip tissue extends beyond the teeth by the same amount for high and low notes regardless of the thickness of the tissue, the length of the lip and the jaw setting.

FAULTS CAUSED BY AN IMBALANCE OF MUSCLE ACTIVITY

- Fault: the lip aperture is too long and too narrow, commonly known as a smile embouchure.

44

Cause: the cheek muscles are overpowering the lip muscles resulting in a spread of the modiolus.

Effect: the sound becomes thin and fragile. Higher notes become sharp. Stamina is lost.

- Fault: the lips are too long for the high note resulting in the tissue extending too far beyond the support of the teeth.
  Cause: the nose and chin muscles failed to shorten the lips when the distance between the teeth was reduced.
  Effect: 'raspberry' tone quality with distinct crackle. No high range.

Players with short teeth and long lips will need to contract their nose and chin muscles more vigorously for high notes. Players with long teeth and short lips will not need to contract their nose and chin muscles quite so vigorously for high notes.

PREPARATION FOR A BALANCED TRANSITION FROM ONE 'SETTING' TO ANOTHER

Perhaps, one of the better ways of rehearsing a balanced transition between a low and a high note is to create a glissando 'buzz' on a mouthpiece. When doing this check in a mirror that:

- the jaw rises progressively
- the lip muscles contract in a circular fashion
- the tissue thins against the support of the teeth
- the nose and chin muscles respectively pull up and down
- the modiolus 'set' does not move.

The reverse is easier. Start on a higher 'buzz' checking in a mirror that:

- the jaw lowers progressively
- the lip muscles slacken progressively to open the aperture
- the lip tissue thickens
- the nose and chin muscles slacken to lengthen the lips
- the modiolus 'set' does not move

The next step is to achieve this same balance of contraction when playing an instrument. Here again, flexibility exercises can be invaluable. Start by slurring to adjacent harmonics.

When this can be achieved without moving the modiolus try to maintain a balanced contraction whilst missing out particular harmonics.

45

7 EXTREMES OF REGISTER

This chapter deals with matters that combine control of the primary resister with control of the three subsidiary resisters.

Question 25	Answers
How do you help your student to play in the extreme, high register?	Leave it to the initiative of the student 90%. Through the use of callisthenics or other similar material 10%

Comment: The spontaneous response from the majority of my interviewees was to leave this aspect of technique to the initiative of the student. However, most qualified this initial statement with comments such as:

- Try to ensure that the normal working range is secure before encouraging a student to experiment with the extreme, high range.
  The brass player has three registers, the high register, the low register and the cash register
- Try to ensure that the student maintains a standard embouchure with breath support when experimenting in the extreme, high register.
- Remind a student to co-ordinate breath, tongue and glottal movements in support of the embouchure muscles.

The 10% using callisthenics or similar material believe that brass playing is an athletic endeavour and, as such, the performer has to expose his muscles to an increasingly demanding situation.

The apparently contrasting responses to Question 25 are not entirely contradictory. The larger group agree that muscle development can only take place when the musculature is properly 'set-up' and cared for. The smaller group agree that muscle development requires exposure to increasingly demanding situations. The differences which emerge between the two groups are towards attitude and timing, and not towards the physical approach.

- The larger group is more cautious and tends to leave this area of technique until quite late in the development of the student.
- The smaller group consider this area of technique should be met 'face-on'. Any problem arising to be dealt with as it occurs.

The following two quotes may also appear contradictory, but again, I believe them to contain complementary advice.

A high note requires an extremely small aperture between the lips. . . this tiny aperture must be resilient and vibratory.

Philip Farkas. The Art of Brass Playing. Wind Music Inc.

Concentrate on using your breath support and **not your lips** *to reach the upper notes. Breathe deeply, anchor the corners to the bottom teeth and keep pressure off top lip.*

Charles Gorham, Bloomington, Indiana.

Farkas states a simple fact. The smaller the lip aperture the higher the note but he qualifies the statement by adding that the tissue must be vibratory. In other words, the lip aperture should not become too small and the lip tissue too firm. This would result in an impaired lip vibration.

Gorham recommends an emphasis on speeding the breath for high note playing. This is not to say that in so doing the player excludes lip contraction. The reverse is true. His statement implies that lip contraction is so much a part of the muscular memory by the time a player is performing in the high register, that thought is no longer required. By concentrating on breath support, anchoring the lip corners and removing as much pressure as is possible from the top lip, the player maintains a resilient and vibratory lip.

Farkas emphasises the lip aperture and Gorham emphasises the contraction of the breathing muscles. The following quote focuses on the use of the mouth aperture:

The tongue-controlled air stream will increase range.

Dr. Charles Colin, Advanced Lip Flexibilities, Charles Colin.

I have been unable to find a quotation that specifically mentions the use of the glottal aperture in relation to high note playing. However, I believe involuntary reduction in the dimension of the glottal aperture, co-ordinates with the reduction of the lip aperture. This occurrence prevents the build-up of breath pressure in the head cavity but also conveniently help the tongue and jaw in compacting the airstream. However, in order to compact the airstream, it is necessary to apply pressure from all directions. So we now arrive at the basic skill of successful high note playing; the co-ordinated effort of each area of resistance. The breathing muscles at one end of the airstream provide the appropriate thrust, the lip aperture at the other end offers appropriate resistance and both are supported in compacting the airstream by the glottal and mouth apertures.

The 'body motions' to be synchronized for high note playing are listed below:

- Raise the 'floor" beneath the lungs to increase the air pressure to well over atmospheric pressure. This will ensure that the air is exhaled at a rapid rate.
- The glottal aperture will reduce involuntarily to maintain breath pressure in the head to an acceptable level. In doing so, this will compact the air.
- Raise both the jaw and the tongue to reduce the mouth aperture. This will accentuate frictional vibration and high overtones. It will therefore compact the air column further and assist in speeding the exhalation.
- Reduce the lip aperture and firm the lip tissue by contracting the lip muscles in a circular fashion. This creates friction which stimulates the red membrane into a rapid vibration.
- Prevent the lip aperture from total closure by contraction of the three groups of face muscles away from the centre of the aperture.
- Apply a little extra mouthpiece pressure. This helps create a seal between mouthpiece and lips.
- Articulate from the hard palate. This focuses on the air column, directing it towards the mouthpiece cup.
- Think positively. This helps synchronize the body motion.

Question 26	Answers	
Do your students use the pedal register?	Yes	35%
	No	65%

48

Question 27	Answers
If your student uses the pedal register, what benefits are derived?	A relaxed red membrane surrounding the lip aperture 60% full lip vibration 40%

Comment: The majority of those answering 'yes' to Question 26 believe that a student gains a relaxed red membrane surrounding the lip aperture through the regular playing of pedal notes. Also, this more relaxed approach would seem to have a beneficial effect on the quality of high note playing.

Those in the other group appear to be making a comment with similar implications. In order to create a full lip vibration it is necessary to achieve the most relaxed red membrane appropriate to the note required.

> *There are two reasons for mastering pedal tones. The first is clinical. The position of the embouchure needed to play a pedal tone is open and relaxed. This is exactly what is needed to play the high notes. The second reason for this study is artistic. The technique gives the performer an extended range that is practical and beautiful.*
>
> *Harold Branch, Pedal Tones for Trumpet, Harold Branch Publications Inc.*

Branch is writing figuratively when he says that the embouchure is required to be open and relaxed for high notes. He is making the important point that the lip aperture should be as open and as relaxed as possible when playing in the high register.

> *The use of these notes in practice will, if properly used:*
> *Correct your embouchure – therefore, help high register*
> *Give you more power and fluency*
> *Aid your attack and sureness*
> *Develop better vibration*
> *Develop intervals and fluency*
> *Bigger sound in all registers*
> *Develop endurance.*
>
> *Claude Gordon, Systematic Approach to Daily Practice for Trumpet. Copyright © 1965 by Carl Fischer Inc. New York*
> *Reprinted by permission, International copyright secured.*

I should like to emphasise one of Claude Gordon's points previously unmentioned. That is the ability to rectify an embouchure fault through the practice of pedal notes. I find this to be particularly effective for a student who has an exaggerated 'smile embouchure'. The playing of pedal notes encourages the formation of a more compact embouchure which precludes the possibility of stretching the obicularis oris muscle into a smile position.

Question 28	Answer
If your student uses the pedal register what guidance do you give?	Push the lower jaw forward and relax the embouchure 100%

The following quotes offer further advice:

> *Play a low F# with all three valves. While you are holding the note, make it go flat, very flat. Notice the feeling you have of forcing this note flat. This is the feel of the pedal F, E, E♭, D & D♭.*
>
> *Claude Gordon, Systematic Approach to Daily Practice for Trumpet. Copyright 1965 by Carl Fischer Inc. New York.*
> *Reprinted by permission. International copyright secured.*

A very relaxed embouchure is needed to produce these notes with plenty of projection of the bottom jaw and lip. Play a low B with a carefully observed 'corners down' embouchure, and aim for the best possible tone-quality. When this is established, make a downward lip glissando, very slowly, until the lower octave is reached. The pedal note will eventually sound on what is basically the same embouchure (except for projected bottom jaw and lip) as the octave above.

Denis Wick, Trombone Technique, OUP.

When playing the pedal

    1. Push the jaw down and out.
    2. Make sure teeth are spread.
    3. The lips should be soft.
    4. The corners should be tight
    5. Be sure to play your normal setting. Do not pucker or unroll your lip.
    6. Play pedals with a lot of air and forte sound.
    7. Do not bob your head down for the pedals.

Harold Branch, Pedal Tones for Trumpet, Harold Branch Publications Inc.

For descending pitches, slight pressure is applied on the lower lip, the lip opening is made larger by a proportionate downward and outward movement of the jaw and lower teeth, the lip muscles are proportionately relaxed, and the air stream is directed more horizontally at a point in the mouthpiece cup closer to the bone.

Gunther Schuller, Horn Technique, OUP

The body motions to be synchronized for pedal notes are listed as follows:

- Lower the 'floor" beneath the lungs but maintain a strong abdominal contraction. Little or no resistance from the diaphragm is required.
- The glottal aperture will increase involuntarily as the lip aperture opens. This will create a broad air stream.
- Lower both the jaw and tongue to increase the mouth aperture. This will reduce frictional vibration and increase the lower overtones by allowing air to resonate throughout the mouth aperture. This will continue to provide a broad 'channel' for the air stream.
- Increase the lip aperture and slacken the lip tissue by relaxing the lip muscle and allowing the lower jaw to open the lips. This reduces friction at the red membrane and creates a slower vibration.
- Prevent the lip aperture from collapsing by holding the modiolus quite firmly.
- Remove all mouthpiece pressure. The mouthpiece will seal with the lips because of the softer lip tissue.
- Articulate from below the top teeth and behind the top lip. This focuses the breath direction towards the bore of the mouthpiece.

Think positively. This helps synchronize the movements.
    All my students work at this exercise:

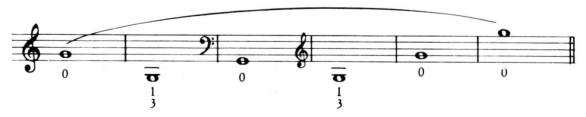

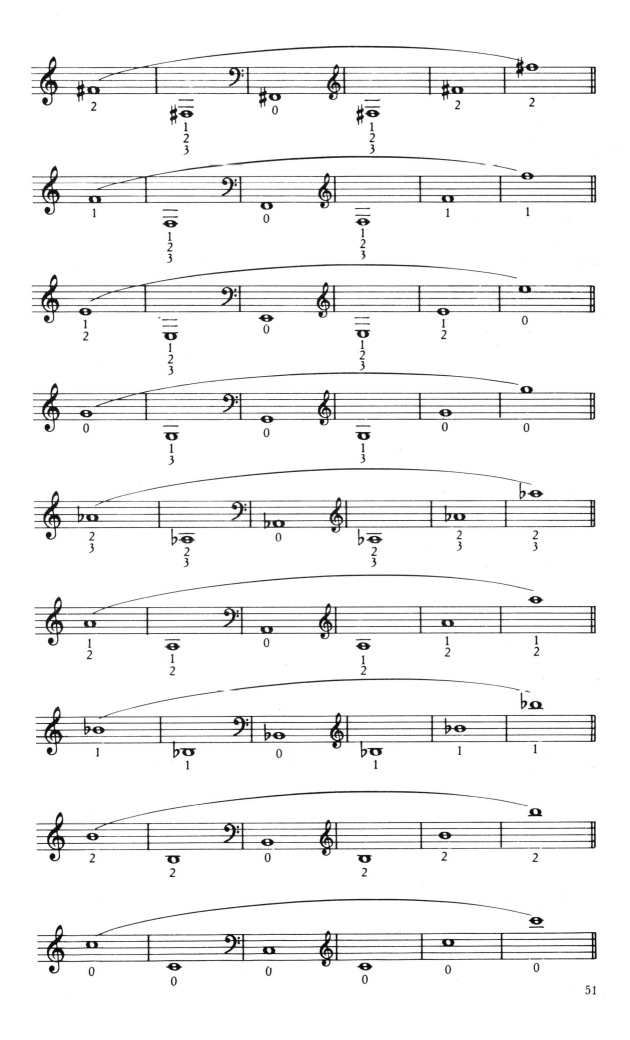

51

Movements of the lip aperture, lower jaw, tongue and instrument in relation to pitch.

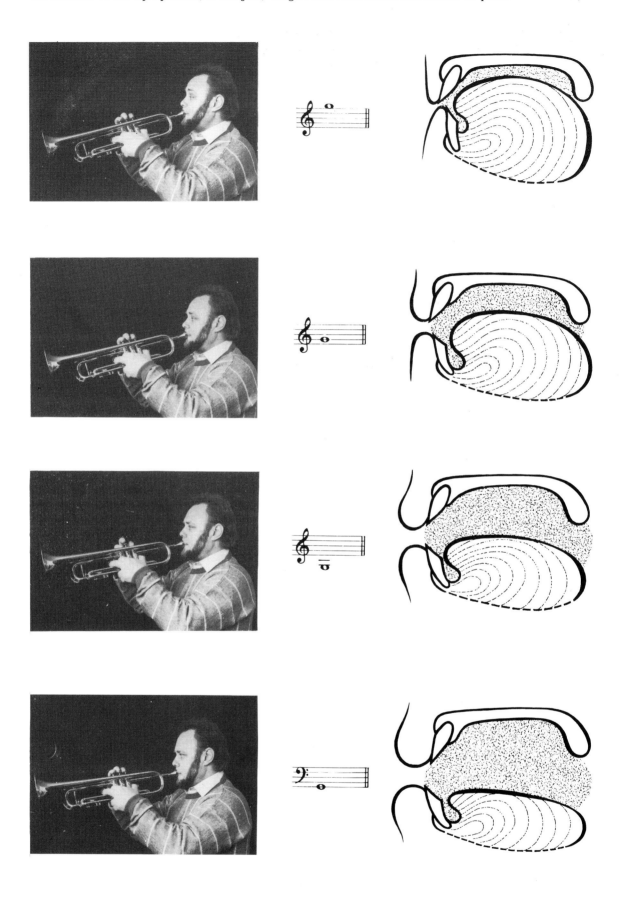

Notice

- The thickening of the lip tissues as the note descends.
- The downward and forward thrust of the jaw and tongue as the note descends.
- The resulting change in the angle of the instrument.

8 LIP MATTERS

This final chapter deals with two aspects of practice which are frequently of concern to students—the warm-up and the development of stamina.

Question 29

Do you encourage students to warm up?

Answer
Yes   100%

Question 30

What purpose is there in a warm up?

Comment: Each of my interviewees was acutely conscious of the athletic element involved in brass playing and consequently encouraged the student to start every practice session with a limbering up routine.

> *Just as the 100-yard specialist needs to start his days training with a gradual limbering-up, so the trombonists too need a very gradual warm-up. I would even go so far as to say that a player who has to perform for any length of time needs to warm up for at least twenty minutes . . . . any short cuts will seriously impair his ability to stay the distance.*
>
> *Denis Wick, Trombone Technique. OUP*

> *The purpose of this loose, free beginning is to wake up the lips. It is something like stretching when one first gets out of bed.*
>
> *Richard Moore & Eugene Ettore, Master Horn Warm-Up and Flexibility Studies. Mel Bay Pub. Inc.*

The following quote recognises that in order for a player to achieve musical sensitivity he must first achieve sensitivity to his muscles.

> *The greatest artist on the french horn that I have been privileged to hear spent a full half-hour warming up each day. It simply took that long for his embouchure and breathing apparatus to reach the degree of sensitivity his great artistry demanded.*
>
> *Gunther Schuller, Horn Technique. OUP*

Despite general agreement that a regular warm-up was necessary, different views were expressed about the nature of this routine and how it should be approached.

> *I purposely avoid the term 'warm-up' as I feel it to be an inaccurate description of what one should do. I prefer to call the method of physical training a 'practical plan'. This will vary according to many different circumstances. . . .*
> *a basic 'warm-up' each day, far from automatically improving playing, may consolidate a great many bad habits. . . . in particular I am concerned that the term 'warm up' implies a certain lazy mental approach to our physical training.*
>
> *Barry Tuckwell, Playing the Horn. OUP*

For many players the typical warm-up consists of a scale or two, a few lip-slurs and perhaps some tonguing – maybe not even this much – all of which takes five minutes or so and is generally played with utter disregard to intonation, rhythm or quality of sound.

Louis Davidson, Trumpet Technique. Pub. Louis Davidson.

For my part, I place great importance on a thoughtful warm-up for three reasons:

- Cold muscles are inefficient.
- Embouchure and breathing muscle irregularities are instantly recognisable during the 'warm-up'. These irregularities can be rectified by a planned, daily routine.
- Correct muscle memories are developed. For this reason, I prefer the exercises to be repetitious and to be performed slowly. Attention is focused by playing with the eyes closed.

Question 31

What 'warm-up' routine do you recommend a student to follow?

Comment: There was a wide variety of response out of which emerged certain similarities in approach:

- The initial lip vibration of a playing session should be gentle
- The initial lip vibration should produce a comfortable note – middle to low register.
- The initial lip vibration should respond to a gentle breath – mezzo-forte.
- The 'warm-up' should be tailored to the state of the embouchure.

The following quotes encompass the above sentiments:

Warm-up rules to Remember.
1. Throat absolutely relaxed; as little motion (while tonguing) as possible.
2. Jaw relaxed; as little motion as possible.
3. Lip tension and
4. Pressure of mouthpiece on lip as little as possible.
5. Air supports tone; Lips are only GUIDES for the air.

If the lips are tense, play low notes. If they are flabby and weak, work slowly up to higher notes but never force a note or apply undue pressure. It is very important that you don't pick up the horn and try to hit a very high or loud note – this can harm the playing for the whole day . . . . or several days. Ease into the days playing slowly and carefully.

Richard Moore & Eugene Ettore, Master Horn Warm-up and Flexibility Studies. Mel Bay Pub. Inc.

To begin with the muscles of the embouchure should be gently stimulated by playing a few notes on the mouthpiece alone. This 'buzzing' as a preparatory exercise can save valuable time; when the warm-up proper starts, on the assembled instrument, the first sounds appear much more easily. These should be the most easily and gently blown notes – middle F or low Bb separated with rests equal in length to each note.

Denis Wick, Trombone Technique. OUP

The removal of the mouthpiece from the lips helps the circulation of the blood after playing a note. There is nothing more injurious to the lips than abusive pressure in the initial 'warm-up'.

Milan Yancich, A Practical guide to French Horn Playing. Wind Music Inc.

The 'warm-up' routine that I recommend to trumpet students is:

'Buzz' on the mouthpiece and check in a mirror that

- The lower jaw is held in its forward position. I find that the lower jaw recedes to its withdrawn position if regular checks are neglected.
- The lip muscle is rounded.
- The three sets of outward contracting muscles are holding the chin and cheeks in a state of gentle firmness.
- The modiolus is 'locking' in the normal position.
- The mouthpiece is correctly positioned.
- The mouthpiece pressure is kept to a minimum.

PLAY:

- Articulate the first note of each phrase with the breath.
- Continue this exercise to the extremity of your range.
- Attempt to extend your range on alternative days. Muscular growth is achieved most effectively by pushing beyond the point of endurance on these days and working within the normal bounds of endurance on the intervening days.
- Concentrate on the muscles involved. Use a mirror to check the embouchure is working correctly on alternative days. Undertake this check in the 'mind's eye" on the intervening day in order to develop muscular memory.

Now Play:

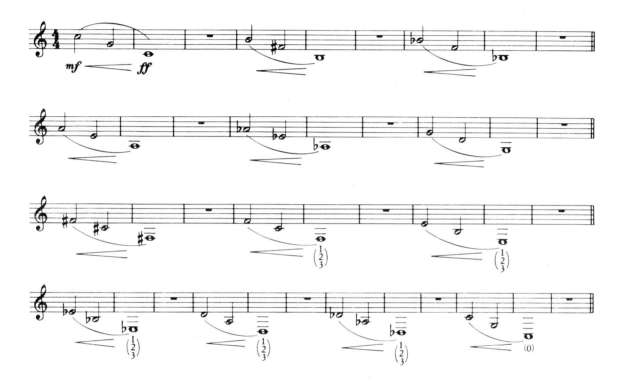

- Articulate the first note of each phrase with the breath.
- Use a minimum of embouchure movement.
- Broaden the air stream to descend by:
  opening the glottal aperture.
  opening the mouth aperture.
  opening the lip aperture.
- Make the lip tissue malleable to descend by:
  removing progressively, the tension from the lip and face muscles.
  thickening the lip tissue.
  removing mouthpiece pressure.

You will have noticed that I omit the 'tongue articulation' from my warm-up routine for those with an insecure embouchure. This avoids the possibility of the lip-tissue being forced into vibration when the lip aperture may not be properly adjusted.

The 'breath articulation', an additional means by which the state of the embouchure can be assessed, should be used during the warm-up, because without the explosive effect of the 'tongue articulation' the lip tissue will only vibrate when the lip aperture is properly adjusted.

For those with a secure embouchure, I recommend that each slurred phrase is instantly repeated with a tongue articulation. This enables the student to match the position of the tip of the tongue with the position of the rear of the tongue in relation to note selecting.

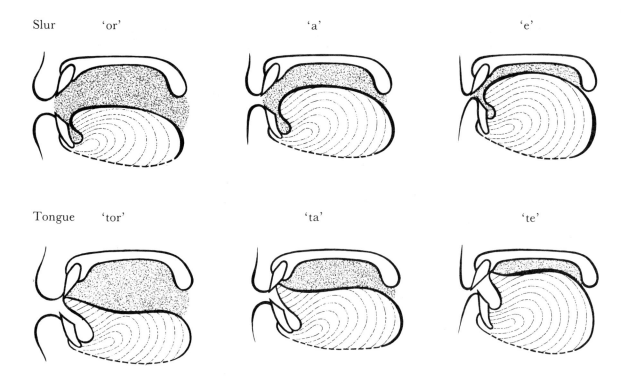

| Slur | 'or' | 'a' | 'e' |
| Tongue | 'tor' | 'ta' | 'te' |

Question 32	Answers
What approach do you adopt when helping a student to develop stamina?	The wide variety of response reflects an emphasis on personal solution. The more common of these solutions are:

- Practice long notes.
- Practice pedal notes.
- Transfer mouthpiece pressure from the top to the lower lip.
- Remove all unnecessary mouthpiece pressure.
- Replace embouchure tension with breath support.
- Expose the embouchure muscles to progressive punishment. Give assistance in establishing a good physiological basis to playing but encourage a personal approach to the development of stamina.

The following quotes represent the attitude of the majority of my interviewees:

The lips will not miraculously get stronger by aimless blowing. They must be developed. It is how you practice that counts.

Our purpose is to strengthen and train muscles not destroy them. Follow these rules:

1. Rest as much as you play.
2. When you are tired, rest.
3. Always take a big breath. This will save your lip muscles.
4. Trumpet playing is a form of athletics. Keep yourself in good physical condition. Keep in training like an athlete.

*Endure until endurance is achieved. . . . . The point at which one finally becomes tired during his practice day is a very valuable moment and should not be wasted. When else can one practice the ability to endure? Therefore, in my case, it is almost a point of honor to go on for another five minutes just when I think I cannot possibly continue. In doing this, I am very careful to use good judgement. The very high notes are avoided, as is fortissimo; but a few minutes of mezzo-forte middle-register notes will not be harmful, and they will give the strength, will power, and confidence that I **can** go on.*

*Philip Farkas, The Art of French Horn Playing. Summy-Birchard Music. Copyright © 1956 Birch Tree Group Ltd.
Used by Permission.*

Stamina is a combination of planned muscular memory development and the calculated conservation of energy. . . . . when most of the obstacles, such as bad co-ordination, pressing, bad posture, or defective breathing have been removed, energy is immediately available for any purpose desired and the player is able to make full use of his body.

Barry Tuckwell, Playing the Horn. OUP

Here are some additional suggestions:
Do
- Play long stretches of music without stopping.
- Play a study without stopping to rest; then, work towards playing that study twice without stopping to rest.
- Play a study at the normal speed without stopping to rest; then, play it at a slower speed.
- Develop stamina appropriate to the demand. One type of performance requires a different kind of strength to another.

Do Not
- Try to gain in stamina on a daily basis.

And finally, don't put your instrument away when you have reached a point of exhaustion. Always finish with a comfortable 'warm-down'.

ACKNOWLEDGEMENTS

Thanks are due to the publishers and authors mentioned below for permission to use quotations within their copyright.

Robert Curry, The Mechanism of the Human Voice. J and A Churchill, Churchill Livingstone, Edinburgh.

D. W. Evans MD and L. C. Lum MB, Hyperventilation as a cause of angina-like pain. Practical cardiology. Med. Publishing Inc.

Donald S. Reinhardt, Pivot system. Reproduced by permission of Elkan-Vogal Inc./UMP Ltd.

Philip Farkas, The Art of Brass Playing. Wind Music Inc.

Philip Farkas, The Art of French Horn Playing. Summy Birchard Music copyright © 1956 Birch Tree Group Ltd. Used by permission.

Barry Tuckwell, Playing the Horn. OUP.

Dr. Charles Colin, Advanced Lip Flexibilities. Charles Colin.

Harold Branch, Pedal Tones for Trumpet. Harold Branch Publishing Inc.

Claude Gordon, Systemetic approach to daily practice for Trumpet. Copyright © 1965 by Carl Fischer, Inc., New York. Reprinted by permission. International copyright secured.

Dennis Wick, Trombone Technique. OUP.

Richard More and Eugene Ettore, Master Horn Warm-up and Flexibility Studies. Used by permission Melbay Publications, Inc.

Gunther Schuller, Horn Technique. OUP.

Louis Davidson, Trumpet Techniques. Pub. Louis Davidson

Milan Yancich, A practical guide to French Horn Playing. Wind Music Inc.

Brass Wind Publications also wishes to thank Michael Gore Browne and Ken Koch for their help in preparing the material for publication.

Printed in Great Britain by
Antony Rowe Ltd., Chippenham